Japanese Dishes
for Wine Lovers

Japanese Dishes
for Wine Lovers

Machiko Chiba

With wine pairing advice by
J. K. Whelehan

Photographs by Tae Hamamura
Translation by Elizabeth Floyd

KODANSHA INTERNATIONAL
Tokyo • New York • London

MEASUREMENTS

1cup = 240 ml	1 inch = 2.5 cm
1 tablespoon = 15 ml	340°F = 170°C
1 teaspoon = 5 ml	350°F = 180°C
1 pound = 450 g	370°F = 190°C
1 ounce = 28 g	400°F = 200°C

Photograph of J. K. Whelehan by Mami Whelehan.
All other photographs by Tae Hamamura.

The publisher would like to give special thanks to Pieroth Japan K.K.

Distributed in the United States by Kodansha America, Inc., and in the United Kingdom and continental Europe by Kodansha Europe Ltd.

Published by Kodansha International Ltd., 17–14 Otowa 1-chome, Bunkyo-ku, Tokyo 112–8652, and Kodansha America, Inc.

First edition, 2005
11 10 09 08 07 06 05   10 9 8 7 6 5 4 3 2 1

www.kodansha-intl.com

CONTENTS

Fish and Seafood 71

Rice and Noodles 101

I guess that my long acquaintance with the United States and my work as a teacher of Japanese cooking actually began back in 1988, when I studied nutrition at the University of Pittsburgh. Later, I also had the opportunity to study cooking in San Francisco, but I think my experience in Pittsburgh was really the beginning, since that is when I began to introduce Japanese cooking to others and to offer classes. Back then, the number of people who were interested in Japanese food was quite limited, as were the images that people had of the cuisine, basically only sushi and tempura. In Pittsburgh, I often taught classes on making sushi. When I look back at the notes I prepared for those classes, I am amazed; the world has changed so much since then.

Time passed and my eldest daughter entered music school in New York City, and so once again my life began to include regular trips to the United States, this time to Manhattan. On one such trip I agreed to begin teaching Japanese cooking in New York, giving me yet another reason to travel back and forth. The connection that I formed to the city during this time was instrumental in laying the foundation for this book.

New York, as everyone knows, is a city that continually absorbs new influences, taking them in stride and moving right along without the slightest pause. For me as a cook, it seems an extraordinarily creative place: a place where you can easily find good food from around the world, and good drink to go with it, and where there is no end of restaurants with intriguing, innovative designs.

It was about four or five years ago that Japanese food started to make a real impact in New York. The number of restaurants increased and menus became much more varied and interesting. At about this same time, people were also becoming more familiar with a wider range of dishes, and pretty soon Japanese ingredients, flavorings, and cooking tools became much easier to find in stores. Silken tofu came on the market, edamame could be found everywhere, and it was possible to buy konbu, shiitake, wakame, hijiki, burdock, and many other items. How changed everything was! Items not found in stores could be ordered online with little trouble, and more Japanese companies were expanding their operations into the United States, making things easier still.

New York was right at the center of the explosion in popularity of Japanese cooking, and it was exciting to be there as a teacher. I began to notice a striking trend in the kinds of dishes that people were drawn to. Aside from taste, they were ones that could be eaten equally well as either a main dish or an appetizer: in other words, not merely food to be served with a big bowl of rice, but food that could stand alone, that was simply prepared, and that went well with wine. This was the kind of food that I found people liked.

The popularity of wine has grown tremendously in the United States over the last decade or two. Wine industry analysts say that consumption of wine is interdependent with variety and richness in the diet. I strongly believe that true variety in diet will always include cuisines of many different countries, including Japan.

Japanese cooking lets the taste of each ingredient emerge. It is not overly spicy, overly sweet, or overly sour. For these reasons it is extremely well-suited to accompaniment by wine.

In this book I introduce a modern version of Japanese food—dishes that are easily prepared and can be eaten on their own, as a kind of appetizer. I have avoided dishes that are hours in the preparation or require complicated processes or tools. I also tried to select low-calorie, healthy dishes.

I want to do away once and for all with the notion that only a dry white wine goes well with Japanese food. I want to show how easy it is to enjoy Japanese food with good wines of every type.

Finally, I would like to express my deep gratitude to J. K. Whelehan, who took charge of the selection and discussion of wines in this book, as well as to his wife Mami Whelehan, whose assistance was invaluable. I am also grateful to my staff for all their help with this book, and to Ginny Tapley and Shigeyoshi Suzuki at Kodansha International.

—MACHIKO CHIBA

PAIRING JAPANESE FOOD AND WINE

In Western society, the roots of the vine had firmly established themselves by the time the Greek and Roman gods of wine, Dionysus and Bacchus, were at their zenith. In Japan, though, legend has it that the vine arrived in 718, passed by Buddha to a holy man called Gyōki, who planted it in what is present-day Yamanashi Prefecture. There is no record of wine being made, however, and the grapes were probably used for the table or medicinal purposes. Instead saké, made from fermented rice, prevailed as the "drink of Gods." Though first brewed in Japan around 300 B.C. as a result of the introduction of wet rice cultivation, its origins in China can be traced as far back as 4,000 B.C.

In those days of old, when wine and food were consumed locally, it was maybe only natural that regional wine and cuisine should complement each other. Even today a basic rule of thumb is to match the wine and dish from the same region. In Japan, the custom of accompanying food with saké likely developed along the same lines as wine in the West, with the local saké complementing the food of the region. As with wine and grapes, different types of rice produce various styles of saké, ranging from dry to sweet, each with its own specific serving temperature. Unlike wine, however, saké is best consumed young and fresh. Being the essence of rice, sake has an added advantage over wine when pairing with Japanese food, especially with dishes like sushi. With wine we cheat to gain such advantage by adding some wine in the cooking process, so for recipes containing saké in this book, such as Salmon Marinated in Saké, you can try substituting saké with wine to improve a match.

By the fourteenth century, mass production of saké heralded its position as Japan's most popular drink. In fact, it wasn't until the sixteenth century and the arrival of the Portuguese, who introduced sugar and corn, that wine consumption was first recorded in Japan. This habit was quickly expelled along with the missionaries, during the Tokugawa Shogunate era (1603–1867).

Also by the sixteenth century, shōchū, Japan's other indigenous drink, started to make an appearance, most likely introduced to Okinawa from Indochina.

Unlike saké, it is a product of distillation, with an average strength of 25%, but sometimes as high as 42%, and is made from raw materials such as rice, grain, sweet potatoes, or raw sugar. Today, while the consumption of saké wanes, shōchū is making a remarkable resurgence, with connoisseurs focusing on the raw materials and regional characteristics.

Commercial winemaking in Japan started in 1875. Wineries of the day faced a myriad of problems, such as a humid climate, inappropriate grapes, and the necessity of dealing with smallholdings, as they themselves were not permitted to own any vineyards. They survived, however, and grapes are now grown in forty-six of the nation's forty-seven prefectures. The most significant grape variety is the Kōshū, which arrived via the Silk Road over 1,200 years ago. Though primarily an eating variety, it has been adopted by Japanese wine producers and typically produces a very pale, light, delicate wine that is generally sweetish, but goes surprisingly well with a broad range of Japanese food.

In Japan, wine has generally been adopted and consumed along with new foods rather than with traditional Japanese cuisine. This is partly due to the influence of restaurants, as well as the unique composition and flavors of the traditional cuisine, with little frame of reference to guide selection. Flavors are subtle, and traditional condiments or seasonings are used to sweeten a dish or increase the "umami," making it challenging to match.

The appreciation of wine and food is affected by appearance, color, smell, taste, temperature, and vehicle of delivery, as well as physiological and psychological factors. Of these, taste is probably the most significant. Typically, most of us are only aware of sweet, sour, salty, and bitter tastes. There is, however, a fifth taste, called "umami," a Japanese word that translates literally as "delicious taste," and is more commonly described as "savory." The source of this taste is glutamate and ribonucleotides. It was identified in 1907 by Professor Kikunae Ikeda, who noted that the widely-used dashi stock made with konbu (dried kelp) had a particular character, so he investigated and discovered that this taste was produced by glutamate. Based on this discovery he developed a new flavoring called monosodium glutamate (MSG). While there has been research to support the concept of umami, it is only recently that researchers at the University of Miami actually isolated a specific taste receptor for it, finally lending it credence.

Umami is a major factor in Japanese food, so it is worth understanding the basic concept. Glutamate and the two ribonucleotides inosinate and guanylate contribute most to the umami taste. It is readily recognized that pairing umami from different sources—that is, glutamate with inosinate or guanylate—increases the effect of umami exponentially. It is also enhanced by natural ripening, fermentation, cooking, smoking, curing, and aging.

This means, for example, that wine from grapes with higher ripeness levels, bottle fermentation, or extended lees contact should have a higher umami content and should therefore marry better with Asian cuisine where umami is

Umami		
Amino acid	Ribonucleotides	
Glutamic acid	Inosic acid	Guanylic acid
Konbu	Chirimenjako	Dried shiitake
Cheese (especially Parmesan)	Katsuobushi	Matsutake mushroom
Soy sauce	Meat	Enoki mushroom
Tomatoes	Fish	
Chinese cabbage	Squid and octopus	

more prevalent and found in higher quantities. This seems to be borne out by the wine and food combinations recommended in this book.

To experience the taste of umami for yourself, add a pinch of MSG to a glass of warm water. Taste and spit out. Then add a pinch of salt to a second glass of warm water and taste. Finally, in a third glass combine both and taste. Combined, the sense of umami is heightened as a result of glutamic acid working synergistically with olfactory sensors and salt, which should mellow the taste and enhance the richness. This should demonstrate how a basic understanding of this fifth taste can help not only to see how taste can be improved, but how it is possible to maximize the effect and bring out the natural flavors of the original dish.

Little has been written in English about umami, and much of what has been written seems misleading. It is often written, for example, that savory foods high in umami make a wine taste drier, less fruity, more acidic, and bitter, with the proposed remedy of adding salt or acid (such as lemon juice) to the food. Yet salt enhances umami! Another common anomaly much stated is that foods high in umami increase the perception of bitterness and create a metallic aftertaste, with oysters being cited as the prime example—even though cheese, so popular with wine, is high in umami!

Under the influence of the Zen monks, who were vegetarian and historically played an important role in developing Japanese cuisine, dried konbu came to prominence as a source of umami and the basis of dashi stock. Konbu is in fact a general term for kelp, of which there are various species, that has gone through a long drying process in order to concentrate the umami. Dashi stock serves a similar function to bouillon, used in Western cooking since 1882, mainly adding umami to various dishes. Instead of meat, which is high in umami, katsuobushi (dried bonito shavings) or dried shiitake are sometimes added along with the konbu to make the dashi.

Soy sauce is another flavoring agent widely used to enhance taste. The original form made from fermented foods dates back to the Yayoi period (300

B.C.–A.D.300), while the soybean version was discovered later in the Kamakura period (1192–1333). Today it is produced from soybeans, which provide the color and umami, and wheat, which adds the aroma and salt.

Being high in lactic acid, soy sauce tends to spin things in favor of red wine. If you wish to experience this for yourself, avocado "sashimi" illustrates it nicely. Indeed, this is one of my favorite dishes because of its simplicity: just slice an avocado, and serve with soy sauce and wasabi. When I tried this, I had maybe ten wines, but all you really need are a light white, a dry rosé, and a light red. You should find that the avocado, when tasted by itself, goes best with rosé, but once you dip it into the soy sauce and wasabi, a lighter red works better.

It is often said that red wine goes with red meat, while white wine is best with white meat and fish. In reality, however, this adage seldom works, as most dishes are accompanied by other ingredients that will actually decide your choice. While soy sauce is certainly a common seasoning, you will find that there are other prominent ingredients in the recipes in this book that will affect your choice of wine. In this respect, mirin, wasabi, shichimi seven-spice pepper, and yuzu citrus are worth understanding.

Mirin was originally meant for drinking, but has been used as a seasoning since the end of the Edo era, when it was particularly popular in the sauces for grilled eel and soba noodles. It was widely adopted as a household condiment in the 1950s. Mirin is made from glutinous rice and distilled spirits (shōchū). It is popular for cooking since it contains approximately 14% alcohol as well as 40–50% sugar, and also has a high concentration of amino and organic acids that contribute to the taste of umami. The alcohol and the succinic acid mask the strong aromas of meat and fish, while the high sugar content causes it to mask the surface of the ingredients to create a sheen. Mirin's inherent sweetness tends to push dishes containing it toward fruity wines, or even wines with some residual sugar, depending on the amount used.

There are three types of mirin: hon mirin, hon naoshi, and mirinfū chōmiryō. Hon mirin is the best quality, and varieties intended for drinking rather than cooking can be as expensive as the best grades of saké. Hon naoshi is a lower grade, in which additional shōchū is added to hon mirin. Mirinfū chōmiryō is the cheapest, being a mixture of grain alcohol, sugars, and flavorings intended for cooking only.

Wasabi is sometimes described as a wine killer. Used properly, however, fresh wasabi should pose few problems. Its roots run deep, being recorded in the oldest herb dictionary from the Heian period (794–1185) when it was also used as a form of tithe. It is used to get rid of fishy smells, increase appetite, suppress germs, and supposedly to prevent cancer. Native to Japan, it is similar to horseradish. Whereas horseradish is typically prepared with cream and served with beef, however, fresh wasabi is simply grated and added to raw fish, raw meat, and some other dishes such as Zaru Soba, or cold buckwheat noodles. When you grind wasabi you should start from the head, where it is more fragrant and spicier. Wasabi is enjoyed for its fragrance, which is best preserved if you can use a wooden grinder and then consume it quickly, as the aroma and spiciness start to dissipate after a couple of minutes. In my experience, the spiciness affects the nose more than the palate, where it does not linger as does chili pepper.

Given its nature, wasabi should not create any major hurdles for wine. Regretfully, though, it is often sold as a paste or powder, which tends to be more potent and thus creates problems for wine. If you cannot get fresh wasabi, remember that only a judicious amount is necessary so that it is just perceptible and not a dominant force. Then, if one observes the correct manner of lightly dipping only the fish in the soy sauce (and never the rice), the fish will become the dominating factor in the choice of wine.

The most challenging condiment is shichimi seven-spice pepper. This was born in 1625 in Edo out of the intention to use Chinese medicinal herbs as food. Though each has its own purported properties, most of these spices or herbs supposedly work to prevent colds, and it seems that the Edoites consumed shichimi for this purpose. The blend in Kantō traditionally matched the propensity for a strong soy sauce flavor with an emphasis on spiciness, while the Kansai blend favored aromatic herbs. Even today, there are differences in the blend depending on the area and individual shops, but a typical example would contain chili pepper, ginger, shiso, sanshō pepper, dried mikan orange peel, black sesame, and hemp seeds. Most commercially-sold brands are categorized into hot, medium, and mild, and the latter is naturally the better choice for wine. Despite the different blends, however, since the main ingredient is chili pepper, shichimi tends to make wine taste bitter.

Organic acids are one of the keys to matching wine and food. One of the most familiar is citric acid, which is found in citrus fruits such as the aromatic yuzu. Native to China, the yuzu came to Japan in the seventh or eighth century. The zest contributes aroma to a dish, while the juice can be used as an alternative to vinegar since it is high in acidity and is more wine-friendly. The acidity in yuzu tends to turn the dish towards white wines with a good acidity, though in both cases overuse should be avoided.

Just as there are specific ingredients in Japanese cooking, there are also certain foods that have become wholly associated with the culture. Probably the most typical food associated with Japan is sushi. The word sushi immediately conjures up an image of raw fish, but the word actually refers to something served with vinagared rice. There are four main categories of sushi today: Nigirizushi (hand-pressed sushi), Makizushi (rolled sushi), Chirashizushi (scattered sushi) and Oshizushi (flat-pressed sushi), all of which have a base of vinegared rice topped variously with raw or cooked fish, seafood, vegetables, or omelet.

Sushi is traditionally partnered with saké and beer. Both work well: saké because it is also made from rice, while beer tends to be fairly neutral with its flavors further muted by its serving temperature, which along with bubbles also helps to refresh the palate. Wine also pairs well with sushi, with Champagne generally being the most versatile, simulating beer while having the added advantage of acidity to cleanse the fishiness (a role traditionally allotted the ginger that accompanies the sushi). Otherwise, though, matching is dependent on the choice of fish.

Sashimi is fresh raw fish or seafood simply sliced and served chilled with wasabi and soy sauce. While freshness is paramount, the style of presentation and cut are equally important. In Japan, sashimi is often purchased ready sliced, or the fish is otherwise clearly marked that it can be used for sashimi. The type of fish used is generally saltwater, since freshwater fish can have parasites that are typically killed by cooking, although there are exceptions, such as carp. Certain types of raw meat are also considered a delicacy, such as chicken and occasionally horse sashimi.

Matching with wine will depend on the fish and, to a certain extent, the season. For example, there are two seasons in which to enjoy bonito, a red meat fish that goes well with red wine and is normally served with a variety of seasonings. In the spring, bonito has less fat and lactic acid. You can use the typical seasonings, but by adding lemon juice and more ginger while going easy on garlic and wasabi, it goes well with dry lighter reds. In the fall, however, bonito requires a heavier red with more tannin, since at this time of year it contains more fat.

Another factor in matching sashimi is how you blend the possible seasonings and herbs. Visiting Kyūshū, I discovered to my surprise that fresh raw squid is actually translucent, and, served simply with salt and a piece of yuzu peel, is excellent with a dry white. In general, squid also goes well with dry white wine if served with soy sauce and ginger, while the traditional soy sauce and wasabi seasoning makes it more red wine-friendly. In summary, first judge whether the fish you choose goes well with white or red wine. If it leans toward whites, and you are drinking white, it is best to choose the condiments that are white-friendly, and vice-versa.

As with any sport, art, or music, one must have a fundamental understanding of the basics to derive maximum pleasure. In this respect, wine and food matching is no different. In this book I have tried to select the best wines to go with the dish with respect to the original recipes. However, there is a school of thought that you should drink any wine you like by balancing the dish to match the wine. This would defeat the point of the book, yet it is important to know the principles. Why? Because although the selection was made objectively, the final choice still remains subjective. Even limiting the wine to a specific vintage and producer does not take into account individual taste or the actual wine selected. By understanding the basic principles, you can compensate and fine-tune the selection to create a better match.

Basically, sweet and savory food makes wine seem drier or less sweet, while fruity tastes make it more acidic and even bitter. This can be counterbalanced by adding acid, such as yuzu, or salt in the form of soy sauce to the food. Dishes on the salty or acidic side, on the other hand, make wine milder, fruitier, less dry, tannic, and bitter. Therefore, by the additional use of a sweet ingredient, such as mirin, you can offset any difficulties.

How does this help? Well, before you start cooking, try the wine. If you discover the wine you selected has a higher or lower acidity than you expected, by adding, for example, more or less yuzu you can counterbalance the deficiency. Similarly, by regulating other ingredients in the recipe, such as saké, mirin, rice vinegar, or soy sauce, you can create a more harmonious match. In some cases you can even change the match by switching the sauce.

In summary, first examine the main ingredients—vegetables, white fish, red meat fish, white meat, red meat, and so on—in order to select a wine to accompany the dish. Secondly, check the seasonings and their amount so you can decide whether the initial choice stands, or whether you have to move toward a white or red. Yakitori is a good example. Chicken is a white meat, and as such goes well with whites, so naturally Yakitori with salt matches very well with white wine, but when you use the sauce containing soy sauce, mirin and sugar, it becomes light red wine-friendly.

Another example lies in the comparison between Steamed Pork and Cabbage with Yuzu and Miso Pork. Both dishes use belly pork, typically matched with heavier whites to reds. In the former dish, since the meat is served with a substantial amount of cabbage and yuzu, which are white-friendly, this dish moves toward light to medium whites. If you also consider sweetness from the steamed cabbage, you will understand why the whites with slight residual sugar go well with this dish. In the latter dish, a substantial amount of soy sauce, mirin, sugar, and miso are used in the marinade. Due to the use of soy sauce and miso, this dish remains a red wine dish, but the sweetness from mirin and sugar makes a possible match with a sweet dessert wine.

When selecting the wines for the recipes in this book, I initially made a paper-match selection based on the ingredients. Then my wife prepared the dishes, and I tasted them with anything up to twenty wines. These selections, then, are made based on dishes that represent home cooking, as opposed to restaurant cooking that is more commonly the source of matches. As a result, the dishes are probably heavier, with more use made of ingredients such as soy sauce, sugar, and mirin. This, however, gave greater scope for wines not normally associated with Japanese cuisine, such as ripe barrel-aged Chardonnays.

Working through the dishes, results were surprising. Sparkling wine without doubt was the most versatile, pairing well with many of the dishes. The bubbles and the cooler serving temperature contribute freshness to many of the dishes—so much so, in fact, that I almost hesitated to include them in certain cases to avoid the selections being totally dominated by this category. On the other hand, two other categories of wines somewhat ignored by me in the past shone through: sparkling red, and halbtrocken.

Most of the dishes tended to be on the sweeter side, especially those that used ingredients such as mirin and sugar. Sparkling red wines, such as Australian Shiraz, Lambrusco, and even a sparkling Malbec from Chili, paired remarkably well with the heavier dishes. One of the problems faced when making sparkling red wines is that the tannins are accentuated by the bubbles and the cold serving temperature. As a result, winemakers leave some residual sugar in the wines to mask the tannins. This way the wine will seem more balanced and smooth, and in fact most people would perceive it as dry. However, this sweetness and the extra weight of the tannins contribute to their success in matching with many of the dishes in this book. For example, the Lambrusco I used was classified as secco (dry), which means legally it can only have from 0 to 15 g/l of sugar. In my case, it contained 10 g/l, which was perfect.

The other category that went extremely well was halbtrocken wine from Germany. To be classified as halbtrocken, the residual sugar should be less than 18 g/l, and no more than 10 g/l greater than the total acidity. Here again, these parameters made for a perfect match in many cases.

Finally, Providence, a red wine from New Zealand, went surprisingly well with a broad range of the dishes, though it did not bear mentioning due to its rarity and cost. Its success lay in having remarkably smooth and integrated or physiologically ripe tannins supported by a balanced acidity. It contrasted with many other wines that have harsh or astringent tannins that would need a solid piece of meat to match with. However, the wine spotlighted nicely the necessity for, and the possibilities of, red wines with soft ripe tannins and a balanced acidity.

Another option regarding the tannins in wine is to look for older wines where the tannins have dissipated over time, giving a supple, rounded wine. This was markedly noticeable when it came to matching with oysters. Surprisingly, the aged Bordeaux, particularly Pomerol, and Burgundy worked remarkably well in this instance. Indeed, with respect to clashes with food, one might wonder about the culpability of tannins over umami!

For those wishing to experience the regional match of Japanese wine and food together, beware of the pitfall I fell into. Make sure the label states "*kokunai san*" which means domestic wine, that is, wine fermented in Japan (the use of imported must or whole grapes is permitted). Avoid those that state "*yūnyū,*" which is made from imported bulk wine, as I learned much to the amusement of a guest who translated the label for me.

And as for umami, well, for now this is probably best taken with a pinch of salt!

—J. K. WHELEHAN

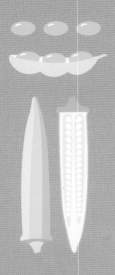

VEGETABLES

TUNA SALAD WITH BURDOCK, CARROT, AND EDAMAME

SERVES 6

1 large burdock root	1 can tuna, 3 1/2 ounces (100 g)
1 medium carrot	1/3 cup mayonnaise
1/2 cup fresh, uncooked edamame	salt and pepper to taste

Cut the burdock into fine matchsticks, then soak in a large bowl of cold water for 10 minutes to remove any astringency, and drain. Cut the carrot into matchsticks. Boil the edamame in their pods for about 10 minutes, and drain. When cool, remove from the pods. Boil the burdock and the carrot for 3 to 4 minutes in a medium saucepan of boiling water just until tender crisp. Remove with a slotted spoon, and drain. Place in a large serving bowl and add the edamame, tuna, and mayonnaise. Mix thoroughly, and sprinkle with salt and pepper to taste.

Beaujolais
Chinon

A light red works well with this dish. I would recommend seasoning the dish with a generous amount of black pepper to widen the options. Indeed, Beaujolais from a good domaine works well, creating a nice balance that allows the taste of the salad to show through. The particular Beaujolais I tried had a distinctive black pepper character, which matched that of the dish. Second choice was a Chinon from the Loire. Produced from Cabernet Franc, the earthy characteristics worked nicely with the burdock and edamame, and the fruit gave dimension, yet as a whole it was light enough not to overwhelm the dish.

WATERCRESS AND CHERRY TOMATO SALAD

SERVES 4

1 bunch watercress, about 1
    ounce (28 g)

20 cherry tomatoes

2 medium potatoes

DRESSING

1 clove garlic, grated

2 tablespoons soy sauce

1 tablespoon sugar

1 tablespoon sesame oil

4 tablespoons vinegar

Rinse and drain the watercress and the cherry tomatoes. Cut the watercress into 1-inch (2 1/2 cm) lengths and cut the cherry tomatoes in half. Rinse the potatoes well, then add to a medium saucepan of boiling water, and boil them in their skins for about 15 minutes, until a fork is pushed through easily. Drain and set aside to cool, then remove the skins and cut into bite-sized pieces. In a small bowl, combine the garlic, soy sauce, sugar, sesame oil, and vinegar, and mix well. Mix together the potatoes, tomatoes, and watercress in a serving dish, and drizzle with the dressing.

Chardonnay
Merlot

The garlic in this dish requires a full-bodied wine from a premium region such as Napa Valley. An oaked Chardonnay from this warmer climate pairs perfectly, especially if it has undergone malolactic fermentation and sur lees aging in the barrel. The latter techniques give the wine a richness that matches the dressing. A rich fruity Merlot also works well, with the sweetness of the fruit matching the flavors of the dish. Avoid Cabernet Sauvignon as it tends to have more tannin, which could clash with the tomatoes.

CRISPY ONION SALAD
WITH CHIRIMENJAKO

SERVES 4

3 ½ ounces (100 g) chirimen-
    jako dried fish

2 medium onions

½ yellow bell pepper

DRESSING

    2 tablespoons soy sauce

    4 tablespoons lemon juice

Place the chirimenjako in a colander and run hot water over them to reduce the fishy smell. Peel the onions, cut them in half lengthwise, and thinly slice. Place the onion slices in a bowl of cold water for 5 to 6 minutes to make them crisp and milder in flavor. Drain well. Rinse the bell pepper and drain; core, seed, and cut into julienne strips. Mix together the chirimenjako, onions, and bell pepper in a small serving bowl. Combine the soy sauce and lemon juice in a small bowl, then pour over the salad and toss well.

Sparkling Wine
Verdicchio

This is not the easiest dish to match with wine due to the dried fish. However, while adding a nice flavor to the dish, the sweetness from the yellow pepper also helps broaden its latitude and dictates a soft round style of wine. A well-rounded sparkler from a warm climate seems to work well as long as the acidity is not too high, so avoid terms such as Brut Zero on the label. Let the bubbles cleanse your palate, not the acidity. Alternatively, a non-oaked fruity white such as a Verdicchio from Italy, produced in a softer modern style, pairs well. Beware that oak tannins will negatively exaggerate the fishy flavors, which are already concentrated in the dried fish.

Champagne
Grüner Veltliner

Pairing wine with this dish is a challenge. Champagne is par excellence an aperitif and ice-breaker, and also very versatile. But first, the key word is Brut (dry). Serving this dish as a starter, I would therefore recommend Champagne as its extra tactile dimension and crisp acidity provides an answer to this and other difficult foods, such as vegetables and eggs, which don't provide a solid, dramatic texture as a foil for the wine. Alternatively Grüner Veltliner, a remarkably versatile wine, matches closest. It has a subtle earthy, mineral character that seems compatible with the carrot, along with weight and acidity to refresh the palate. Whatever you choose, I would recommend a dry wine, with no oak, and with a refreshing acidity.

GRATED MOUNTAIN YAM AND CARROT

SERVES 4

1 yamaimo mountain yam, about 7 ounces (200 g)

1 medium carrot
dash soy sauce

Peel the mountain yam and carrot. Place them together in a food processor and puree until smooth. Pour into small decorative glasses and top each with a dash of soy sauce.

Variations on this recipe can be made by substituting the carrot with ½ ounce (14 g) of either cucumber or parsley.

BROCCOLI AND CAULIFLOWER
CRABMEAT SALAD

SERVES 4

1 head broccoli, about 6 ounces (170 g)

½ head cauliflower, about 11½ ounces (320 g)

5 ounces (140 g) fresh crabmeat, cooked

DRESSING

2 tablespoons soy sauce

2 tablespoons mirin

1 teaspoon sesame oil

2 teaspoons sugar

2 teaspoons vinegar

Break the broccoli and cauliflower into florets. In a large pot of boiling water, blanch the broccoli florets for 3 to 4 minutes and the cauliflower florets for 5 to 6 minutes. Place in a colander and cool under cold running water, then drain. Place the broccoli and cauliflower in a large bowl. Add the crabmeat, flaking it by hand. Combine the soy sauce, mirin, sesame oil, sugar, and vinegar in a small bowl, then pour over the salad and toss well.

Riesling
Koshu

The dressing on this salad is gentle, but also quite sweet. If your philosophy is to match like with like, meaning with a similar weight or body, Koshu from Japan is an identical match. The guidelines here are for some residual sugar, gentle flavors, and a soft mouth feel. For me, though, a halbtrocken Riesling is sublime, as it creates an extremely smooth velvety mouth feel due to the residual sugar, which is then lifted by the inherent citrus character and acidity of the variety.

JAPANESE MUSHROOM TERRINE

SERVES 8

3 ½ ounces (100 g) maitake mushrooms

3 ½ ounces (100 g) shimeji mushrooms

2 tablespoons butter

3 ½ ounces (100 g) shiitake mushrooms, roughly chopped

1 tablespoon soy sauce

1 orange bell pepper, sliced

16 okra

FILLING

3 ounces (80 g) chicken breast

½ egg

3 ½ ounces (100 cc) fresh cream

2 ounces (56 g) cream cheese

1 chicken bouillon cube

dash sugar

Preheat the oven to 340°F (170°C). To prepare the filling, cut the
chicken into bite-sized pieces. Place the egg, chicken, cream, cream
cheese, bouillon cube, and sugar in a food processor, and mix well.
Next break the maitake mushrooms and shimeji mushrooms into small
bunches. Melt the butter in a large frying pan, add all the mushrooms
and stir-fry until soft. Add the soy sauce, reduce the heat to low, and
simmer for 4 minutes to set the flavor. Remove from heat and allow
to cool, then squeeze out any excess moisture. Rinse the bell pepper
and drain; core, seed, cut in half lengthwise, and then cut into half-
inch strips. Rinse the okra and remove the stalks. In a buttered casserole dish, spread a layer of the creamy chicken filling, then alternate
it with layers of vegetables: bell pepper, okra, and mushrooms, finish-
ing up with a layer of filling on top. Bake in the oven for 15 minutes.

Despite the simplicity of the
chicken, the combination of
ingredients link together to create a rich, creamy dish, with the
mushrooms adding a delicious
texture. Though still requiring a
white, a more substantial wine is
called for, such as a barrel-aged
Chardonnay. If you try one from
Chili, look for Reserva on the
label, as the soft ripe fruit matches
the slight sweetness of this dish.
My ideal match, though, was a
Chardonnay from Burgundy, a
Corton Charlemagne Grand Cru
from a riper vintage. The dish
thus transformed became extremely elegant, with the rich
textures of both creating a synergy, while the balanced acidity
gives a lift. A Meursault Premier
Cru from a good vintage may
provide a more affordable match.
(As a general rule of thumb,
despite a myriad of appellation
names, whites from Burgundy are
produced from Chardonnay.)
Needlees to say, a sparkler will
also weave its magic.

KABOCHA SALAD

SERVES 4

1/4 kabocha squash, about
    8 ounces (220 g)

3 tablespoons mayonnaise

2 tablespoons fresh cream

1/2 teaspoon sugar

Using a knife, remove parts of the peel here and there from the kabocha, then cut the kabocha into large bite-sized pieces. Fill a medium-sized pot half full with water, add the kabocha pieces, and boil for 15 minutes, then drain and allow to cool. Combine the mayonnaise, cream, and sugar in a bowl, then add the kabocha and toss well. Arrange on a serving plate and garnish with a few kabocha leaves, if available.

Pinot Gris
Dessert Wine

On top of the kabocha's naturally sweet flavors, you have mayonnaise and fresh cream giving a dish that is quite sweet. Halbtrocken wines from Germany work well, but avoid Rieslings as their inherently high acidity doesn't work. Pinot Gris also pairs well when produced in a rich riper style from California or New Zealand. A tip for the avant-garde: if you are the type of person who puts black pepper on your ice cream, maybe try serving this as a dessert with a "sticky," as the dessert wines from Australia and New Zealand are known locally, but again be sure to avoid those with excessive acidity.

AVOCADO TOFU SALAD

SERVES 4

1 avocado

1 package silken tofu, about 11
    ounces (300 g)

baby leaf greens

DRESSING

wasabi (to taste)

2 tablespoons soy sauce

2 tablespoons dashi stock (see
    page 114)

1 teaspoon vinegar

1 teaspoon mirin

Remove the skin and pit of the avocado, and cut the flesh into ½-inch
(1 cm) cubes. Hold the tofu upside down against a paper towel to
drain some of the moisture from it. Pat dry and cut into ½-inch (1 cm)
cubes. Combine the ingredients for the dressing in a small
bowl. Arrange the avocado and tofu on a serving
plate, garnish with the baby leaf greens,
and drizzle with the dressing.

Sauvignon Blanc
Pinot Gris

This dish is remarkably versatile,
so much so that I would make
the wine selection based on
accompanying dishes. Though
the sauce seems salty, integrated
with the other ingredients it
becomes mild. Sauvignon Blanc,
with its typical herbaceous character, enhances the vegetables,
while a Grüner Veltliner matches
the strength of the avocado. My
preference would be for a ripe
Pinot Gris, with a subtle touch
of oak. From a good producer, it
can have a slight syrupy texture
with almost sweet fruit which
interacts nicely with the slightly
sweet flavors of the tofu. However, if it is good tofu that you
wish to accentuate, try a slightly
sweet, no-oak white, like a Koshu
from Japan. With the avocado,
there is potential for rosé or even
light reds, such as a dry fruity
Lambrusco or a Beaujolais, though
the vegetables will pay a price.

PAN-FRIED TOFU STEAKS

SERVES 4

1 cup mixed dried beans

1 package silken tofu, about
 11 ounces (300 g)

1 tablespoon potato starch
 (or cornstarch)

2 tablespoons olive oil

3 tablespoons soy sauce

3 tablespoons mirin

1 tablespoon sugar

3 tablespoons water

Soak the beans overnight in a bowl of water. Rinse, then boil in a large pot of water for about 1 hour, until a bean pressed between the fingers is easily mashed, then drain. Sprinkle the tofu all over with potato starch (do not drain the tofu). Heat the oil in a frying pan, add the tofu, and fry until both sides are golden. Add the soy sauce, mirin, sugar, and water to the frying pan, and heat until the mixture thickens. Arrange some of the beans around the edge of a serving dish, leaving the center open. Place the tofu in the center of the dish. Scatter the remaining beans around and cover with any left-over sauce from the pan.

Lambrusco Secco
Sparkling Wine

The most important feature is the sauce, which is quite strong and sweet and dominated by soy sauce. It is the key to matching, as the flavor of the tofu is subtle. A Lambrusco Secco (dry) was perfect. Surprisingly, perhaps, Lambrusco so labeled can actually have up to 15 g/l sugar. The wine I tasted had only 10 g/l, which was just right to offset the sweetness of the sauce. Additionally, its fruity nature contributed to the flavors while the bubbles and serving temperature of typically 43°F (6°C) added freshness. A sparkler from Argentina, being both round and fruity, offered a formidable alternative.

ENOKI MUSHROOMS AND
GREEN ONIONS WRAPPED IN BACON

SERVES 4

8 green onions

1 package enoki mushrooms,
   about 3 ½ ounces (100 g)

4 slices bacon

1 tablespoon olive oil

Cut the onions into 2-inch lengths, and cut off the hard portion at the end of the cluster of enoki mushrooms. Cut the bacon slices in half to make 8 pieces. Roll a piece of bacon around a small amount of onion and enoki, and secure with a toothpick. Continue with the remaining onion, enoki, and bacon to make 8 rolls. Heat the olive oil in a frying pan, add the bacon rolls, and cook, turning often.

❙ Bacon is salty, so no flavoring is needed.

Pinot Noir
Garnacha

The flavors in this dish are quite strong due to the combination of green onions and bacon, the latter ingredient also making the dish quite oily. A medium-bodied Pinot Noir from a warmer climate will have sufficient weight and structure to match and, with its typical slightly smoky character, Pinot interacts nicely with the bacon. Spain is now producing some great Garnachas in a modern style. Typically this variety produces wines with light color, high alcohol, and polished tannins. Youthful, fruity, and spicy after a couple of months aging in barrels, they can complement as opposed to dominate, as they are not too heavy. Their aromas and flavors of ripe fruit, pepper, and even coffee are complementary, while the alcohol gives them enough substance.

DAIKON RADISH GYOZA

SERVES 6

18 thin slices daikon radish

10 medium shrimp

3 tablespoons potato starch
   (or cornstarch)

2 tablespoons olive oil

1 cup water

DIPPING SAUCE

3 tablespoons soy sauce

1 tablespoon vinegar

dash rāyu hot pepper oil

Boil the daikon slices in a pot of water until they become transparent, drain, and allow to cool. Shell and devein the shrimp, and chop roughly. Place some pieces of shrimp in the center of each daikon slice, sprinkle potato starch around the edge, fold the daikon over, and pinch-pleat the edges into five overlapping pleats, creating a shell with gathers on top. Heat the oil in a frying pan, add the daikon gyoza, and fry until golden on both sides. Add the water to the pan and simmer on medium heat until the liquid is absorbed, then arrange on a serving plate. Combine the soy sauce, vinegar, and rāyu to make the dipping sauce.

Sparkling Wine
Ermitage (Marsanne Blanc)
AOC Valais

Coarsely minced shrimp adds an interesting texture, contrasting nicely with the daikon radish. They combine to give a gentle texture and flavor offset by the pronounced sauce. The ever-versatile sparkler works well, though a trocken sekt sets the pace. An Ermitage (Marsanne Blanc) AOC Valais is the gourmet's choice. With an ever-so-slight hint of bitterness, the wine is strong enough to cope with the sauce, yet does not kill the gentle flavor of the ingredients. Spanish rosé works with the sauce in particular, creating a synergy, though the delicateness of the ingredients is lost in translation.

MUSHROOMS AND OKRA SAUTÉED IN BUTTER AND SOY SAUCE

SERVES 4

2 eringi mushrooms

5 shiitake mushrooms

3 ½ ounces (100 g) shimeji mushrooms

3 ½ ounces (100 g) maitake mushrooms

2 tablespoons butter

1 clove garlic, minced

1 tablespoon soy sauce

4 okra

dash black pepper

Lightly rinse all the mushrooms in a colander and pat dry with a paper towel. Cut the eringi mushrooms in half and then into thin julienne strips. Cut the shiitake into thin julienne strips. Break the shimeji and maitake mushrooms into small bunches. Melt the butter in a large frying pan. Add the garlic and sauté until fragrant, then add the mushrooms and stir-fry until soft. Pour the soy sauce around the edge of the pan so that the flavor spreads evenly through the mushrooms. Cook on medium to low heat for another 3 minutes. Boil the okra briefly and immediately drain. Cut in half lengthwise, and serve alongside the mushrooms. Sprinkle with pepper to taste.

Chardonnay
Tempranillo

While the eringi mushrooms add a nice texture, the flavors of the garlic and butter are pronounced. A rich barrel-aged, buttery Chardonnay matches the butter, so look for ones that have undergone malolactic fermentation and bâtonnage (stirring of lees). Light reds work well, such as a Crianza from Rioja, which gives freshness to the dish while the fruit adds dimension. Alternatively, the mushrooms bring out the varietal characteristic of Cabernet Franc from the Loire, known as Chinon, highlighting its slightly earthy overtones. The key is to select a light red with a good acidity that can cope with butter, but avoid tannic reds as they will clash with the mushrooms.

HARUMAKI

SERVES 8

4 sheets rice paper wrappers

1 avocado

1 cucumber

1 carrot

4 lettuce leaves

7 ounces (200 g) fresh crabmeat

DIPPING SAUCE

3 tablespoons vinegar

2 tablespoons soy sauce

2 tablespoons mirin

dash rāyu hot pepper oil

Spread out a moistened paper towel and lay one rice paper wrapper on top. Repeat this for all the wrappers, stacking them together. Peel the avocado, remove the pit, and cut into thick slices ½ inch (1 cm) by 2 inches (5 cm). Cut the cucumber and the carrot into 2-inch (5 cm) matchsticks. Flip over the stack of paper towels and wrappers, and begin with the wrapper that is now on top. Place a lettuce leaf, some crabmeat, a piece of avocado, and some carrot and cucumber matchsticks on the wrapper, roll over once, fold the ends down toward the center, and roll again. Cut each harumaki in half to make two rolls, and arrange on a serving plate. Combine the vinegar, soy sauce, mirin, and rāyu for the dipping sauce.

Stacking the rice paper wrappers between moistened paper towels will keep them moist and prevent them from breaking when they are rolled.

Brut Rosé
Sparkling Red

The crab, being a crustacean and here supported by vegetables, suggests a white. The addition of soy sauce and rāyu definitely makes the dish more red-friendly. However, while avocado leans towards red, it pairs best with rosé. So, overall, a brut rosé is ideal as it can tolerate the rich flavors. A more full-bodied style is preferable as the sauce has quite strong ingredients, such as soy sauce, vinegar, and red pepper oil. An option could be to replace the crab with tuna, in which case try some sparkling red from Australia, since tuna and avocado go extremely well with reds and you are always safe with versatile fizz.

JAPANESE-STYLE NAMUL MARINATED VEGETABLES

SERVES 4

11 ounces (300 g) kogomi
   ostrich ferns

1 large carrot

1 bunch fresh spinach,
   about 7 ounces (200 g)

1 yellow bell pepper

1 red bell pepper

fresh bean sprouts, about
   11 ounces (300 g)

FLAVORING

KOGOMI OSTRICH FERNS

2 tablespoons sesame oil

2 tablespoons sugar

3 tablespoons soy sauce

2 tablespoons water

grated garlic to taste

1 tablespoon roasted
   ground sesame seeds

kochijan spicy miso to
   taste

SPINACH

1 tablespoon sesame oil

1 tablespoon soy sauce

1 tablespoon roasted
   ground sesame seeds

dash salt

BEAN SPROUTS

1 teaspoon soy sauce

1 clove garlic, grated

1 tablespoon roasted
   ground sesame seeds

dash salt

Kogomi ostrich ferns: heat the sesame oil in a wok or large frying pan. Add the kogomi ostrich ferns and stir-fry for 1 to 2 minutes. Add sugar, soy sauce, water, grated garlic (to taste), ground sesame seeds, and kochijan miso (to taste). Bring to a boil, then lower the heat and simmer for 4 to 5 minutes until the liquid is reduced by half.

Carrot: cut the carrot into matchsticks, and boil briefly in salted water until tender crisp, then drain.

Spinach: blanch the spinach quickly, removing it from the water before it softens. Drain and squeeze out the excess moisture, then cut into 2 inch (3 cm) lengths. Place in a small bowl, add the sesame oil, soy sauce, ground sesame seeds, and salt, and mix well.

Yellow and red bell peppers: core and seed the bell peppers and cut into strips 1/4 inch (5 mm) wide. Blanch quickly in boiling water, removing from the water before they soften; drain.

Bean sprouts: sprinkle the bean sprouts with salt; blanch briefly in boiling water, removing from the water before they soften. Place them in a bowl and add the soy sauce, garlic, ground sesame seeds, and salt; mix well.

Arrange all the vegetables in strips on a flat square serving dish.

Merlot
Sparkling Wine

A fruity bubbly from a warmer climate is the ideal choice. Its extra tactile dimension provides the perfect answer to this dish as the vegetables do not provide a solid, dramatic texture as a foil for the wine. While the bubbles elevate the dish, the fruit character matches harmoniously with the sweetness of the carrots. If you wish to use a red wine, pick one of the sweet, riper styles of Merlot from California. Being from a warm region, these typically have a lower acidity and high alcohol, which will enhance the sweetness and mouth-feel, creating more background for the dish, while the ripe integrated tannins will not interfere with the texture of the vegetables.

DEEP-FRIED EGGPLANT
WITH SESAME SAUCE

SERVES 6

3 Japanese eggplants

oil for deep-frying

1 tablespoon fresh ginger root,
    grated

10 kinome sprigs for garnish
    (optional)

SAUCE

1 tablespoon sesame paste

2 teaspoons soy sauce

1/2 tablespoon sugar

1 tablespoon water

Cut the eggplants into slices 1¼ inch (2 cm) thick, and pat the slices completely dry with a paper towel. Deep-fry the slices until heated through in a pan of oil heated to 350°F (180°C). Eggplant is done if a skewer passes through it easily. Remove from oil and drain on paper towels. To make the sauce, combine the sesame paste, soy sauce, sugar, and water in a small saucepan and heat on low, stirring with a wooden spoon, until the mixture thickens. Arrange the eggplant slices on a plate and top them with the sesame sauce and grated ginger. Garnish with the kinome sprigs.

To retain skin color, eggplant can also be prepared in a microwave oven. Brush each slice well with olive oil, place on a microwave-safe dish, cover, and microwave for 3 minutes.

Sparkling Wine
Tempranillo

The sesame paste enhances the slightly neutral character of the eggplant. A fruity sparkler works well, the fresh fruit enhancing and lifting the dish while its extra tactile dimension provides an answer to the eggplant which does not present a solid, dramatic texture as a foil for the wine. If you go easy on the ginger, Rioja is a Spanish alternative, with mellow, oaky, vanilla reds made from Tempranillo. The characteristic sweet vanilla, typically coming from the American oak barrel, marries well with the sweetness of the sauce. Choose a young Crianza, as you are also looking for primary fruit flavors to give the dish dimension and freshness.

TOMATO AND ONION SALAD

SERVES 4

½ onion, minced

2 large tomatoes

DRESSING

2 tablespoons mayonnaise

1 tablespoon olive oil

1 tablespoon mirin

1 tablespoon vinegar

Soak the minced onion in a bowl of water for 5 or 6 minutes, and drain well. Cut each tomato into eight pieces, and arrange them on a plate. Top each tomato slice with minced onion. Combine the mayonnaise, olive oil, mirin, and vinegar to make the dressing, and pour over the tomato and onion.

Sauvignon Blanc
Gewürztraminer

This dish requires a wine that can lift it and give it dimension. What is needed is a white wine with a strong varietal character, or even bubbles with their extra tactile dimension. However, avoid those with oak aging. The dish itself is mild and gentle, with the tomatoes and onions in this case contributing sweetness that is further augmented by the dressing. A wine like Sauvignon Blanc with a vibrant acidity gives the dish a certain verve, while the forward fruit-driven aromas broaden its dimension. Similarly, the strong flavors of the Gewürztraminer work well, especially if the onions are piquant. In this case, though, it is primarily the residual sugar that links the wine to the dish as opposed to the acidity.

MEAT AND POULTRY

THIN-SLICED
MARINATED BEEF

SERVES 6

2 tablespoons olive oil

4 cloves garlic, thinly sliced

1 pound 5 ½ ounces (600 g) round
   cut of beef

1 carrot

1 cucumber

1 stalk celery

MARINADE

⅔ cup (160 cc) soy sauce

½ cup (120 cc) vinegar

4 tablespoons (60 cc) mirin

DIPPING SAUCE

2 tablespoons miso

1 ½ tablespoons sugar

1 tablespoon water

Preheat the oven to 350°F (180°C). Heat the olive oil in a medium frying pan, add the garlic slices, and sauté until fragrant. Add the beef to the frying pan and sauté until browned all over. Transfer the meat to a cooking sheet, and bake in the oven for 20 minutes. Combine the soy sauce, vinegar, and mirin in a small bowl to make the marinade. Remove the meat from the oven and place it in a deep-sided dish. Add the marinade, and marinate for 6 to 8 hours, or overnight. Remove the meat from the marinade, and thinly slice. Cut the vegetables into sticks. Combine the miso, sugar, and water, and serve as a dipping sauce for the vegetables to accompany the beef.

Zinfandel
Shiraz

The classic combination for beef is a full-bodied red, especially when combined with a garlic marinade, as here. Zinfandel, a variety adopted by California, produces a full-bodied wine packed with ripe, almost sweet fruit flavors and supple tannins. The characteristically high alcohol content typically augments the perception of sweetness in the wines. As the marinade and dipping sauce also contain sugar and mirin, Zinfandel meets the bill, although a full-blooded Shiraz would measure up nicely. If you use a less fatty part of beef, maybe try a heavy Merlot from California.

Shiraz, from a hot climate, is typically full-bodied, powerful, and alcoholic, with aromas and flavors frequently of pepper, mixed spice, game, and leather, accompanied by a solid core of berry fruit. These inherent qualities both cope with and complement the strong flavors of this dish. The key ingredient in this case is the pepper. In addition, the fattier the beef the heavier the wine should be. Also keep in mind Syrah-based wines from the Rhône Valley, categorized by appellation as opposed to variety, namely Côte-Rôtie or Hermitage. Heavy full-bodied reds, like Cabernet Sauvignon or Californian Zinfandel, should also marry well.

BITE-SIZED PEPPER STEAKS

SERVES 6

- 2 tablespoons coarse-ground black pepper
- 2 beef steaks (rib roast or rib eye roast), about 1 pound (450 g)
- 1 tablespoon olive oil
- 1 clove garlic, minced

- 1 ½ tablespoons sugar
- 4 tablespoons (60 cc) mirin
- 2 ²/₃ tablespoons (40 cc) soy sauce
- 3 buckwheat leaves (or cress leaves) for garnish

Pat the coarse-ground black pepper onto both sides of the beef until the meat is well coated. Heat the olive oil in a large frying pan, add the garlic, and sauté until fragrant. Add the meat and cook until browned on both sides. Add the sugar, mirin, and soy sauce, and cook until the liquid thickens and coats the meat. Cut the meat into bite-sized cubes and arrange on a serving dish. Garnish with the buckwheat or cress leaves.

STIR-FRIED GROUND BEEF AND VEGETABLES WITH OYSTER SAUCE

SERVES 4

SAUCE

- 2 tablespoons saké
- 2 tablespoons soy sauce
- 4 tablespoons oyster sauce
- 2 tablespoons sugar
- 1/2 cup (120 cc) chicken broth
- salt and pepper to taste

- 1 medium onion
- 1 fresh (or canned) bamboo shoot, about two-inches long
- 3 fresh shiitake mushrooms
- 1 medium carrot
- 1 stalk celery
- 1/2 green bell pepper
- 1/2 red bell pepper
- 1 tablespoon olive oil
- 8 ounces (220 g) ground beef
- 2 tablespoons cornstarch, dissolved in a small amount of water
- 1 teaspoon sesame oil
- 2 fresh endives

To make the sauce, combine the saké, soy sauce, oyster sauce, sugar, chicken broth, and salt and pepper in a small bowl, mix well, and set aside. Chop all the vegetables, except the endive leaves. Heat the olive oil in a wok or large frying pan and add the beef. Fry until the meat begins to brown, then add the chopped vegetables and the sauce to the wok. When the vegetables are cooked, add the dissolved cornstarch to the sauce to thicken it. Add the sesame oil and mix. Arrange the endive leaves on a serving dish, and spoon the beef and vegetable mix on top of each.

Merlot
Zinfandel

Merlot tends to ripen earlier than Cabernet and, also with a thinner skin, it normally gives rounder, riper, less tannic wines with softer, juicier, plumper fruit flavors and aromas. This dish is ideally matched with a medium-bodied Merlot, as ground beef tends to be on the fattier side. Combined with sweetness from the oyster sauce, sugar, and vegetables, this requires the riper fruit flavors typical of Merlot. In general you should look for a fruity, medium-bodied red from a warmer climate that is neither acidic nor tannic. A Zinfandel would fit the bill nicely.

BEEF WITH WHITE SESAME AND MIRIN

SERVES 6

½-inch (1½ cm) thick beef steak
(roast cut), about 1 pound (450 g)

2 slices orange, for garnish

SESAME SAUCE

2 eggs

½ cup ground white sesame
seeds

1 tablespoon mirin

3 tablespoons soy sauce

1 tablespoon sugar

Preheat the oven to 350°F (180°C). Cut both sides of the beef steak into diamond patterns ⅛ inch (3 mm) deep. Place in a small ceramic casserole dish. Break the eggs into a bowl and beat well. Add the sesame seeds, mirin, soy sauce, and sugar, and mix well. Pour this mixture over the meat, and cook uncovered in the oven for 15 to 20 minutes. When cool, cut the meat into 2-inch (5 cm) square pieces, and serve.

The cuts in the beef will keep it from curling as it cooks, so the egg mixture can set into a flat layer on top.

Carmenère
Merlot

The Japanese title of this recipe translates literally as "Grilled Beef Rikyū style." Sen no Rikyū (1522–91) was a legendary tea master who supposedly liked sesame seeds, and many recipes containing white sesame are named after him. Sesame is certainly quite dominating in this dish. Because the recipe calls for mirin, soy sauce, and sugar, one might assume it to be on the sweeter side, but this is not the case. As a result it goes well with a range of ripe, fruity reds with soft tannins from warmer climates. A top notch Carmenère, a variety that has now vanished from Bordeaux but which flourishes in Chili, was my choice. It enhanced the sesame flavors in the dish, while its flavors were strong enough to persist on the finish. Check for Reserva on the label. A Merlot from Napa Valley would work equally well.

BEEF AND ORANGE ROAST

SERVES 6

MARINADE

2 tablespoons soy sauce

2 tablespoons sugar

2 tablespoons mirin

2 tablespoons orange liqueur

juice of 2 oranges

1 pound 5 ½ ounces (600 g) beef (khal bi Korean barbecue meat or skirt cut)

2 medium oranges

Preheat oven to 400°F (200°C). To make the marinade, combine the soy sauce, sugar, mirin, orange liqueur, and orange juice in a small bowl. Cut the beef into bite-sized chunks and spread out in a large shallow dish, then pour the marinade over it. Allow the meat to marinate 30 minutes. Cut each orange into 6 or 8 sections. Arrange the meat and orange sections on a cooking sheet, add the marinade, and roast in the oven for 20 minutes, until slightly brown.

Malbec
Lambrusco

Beef and Malbec have both become synonymous with Argentina. Originally from Bordeaux, Malbec is inherently tannic and acidic, yet in the climate of its adopted home it produces wines with less acidity and riper, richer fruit, accentuated by a higher alcohol content. The protein in the meat absorbs the tannins in this wine, an effect similar to that of adding milk to black tea. As a result the wine becomes softer, while the concentrated, almost sweet fruit character, highlighted by the alcohol, bears up to the sauce and creates a perfect foil for the dish. Alternatively, a Lambrusco works well with the inherent sweetness found even in a secco, or dry, version matching that of the dish to create a perfect symmetry.

MISO PORK

SERVES 6

1 pound 5 1/2 ounces (600 g) belly
   pork

MISO SAUCE
   2/3 cup (160 cc) soy sauce
   3 tablespoons sugar

4 tablespoons miso
5/6 cup (200 cc) mirin
10 slices pickled ginger
3 naganegi (or green onions),
   cut into 1 1/2-inch (4 cm)
   lengths

Combine the soy sauce, sugar, miso, mirin, and ginger in a large mixing bowl, mix well, then add the naganegi. Cut the pork in half, and
marinate in the miso sauce for about half a day, or overnight. Heat
the oven to 350°F (180°C). Place the meat and about half the miso
sauce in an ovenproof dish, and cook for 40 minutes. As the meat is
cooking, turn it several times as necessary, and baste with a little of
the remaining miso sauce each time. When the meat is done, remove
from the oven and slice thinly. Pour any remaining sauce over the
meat, and serve.

PORK AND PLUM STIR-FRY

SERVES 6

10 ounces (280 g) pork shoulder

1 tablespoon olive oil

4 large umeboshi pickled plums, with pit removed

1 teaspoon sugar

1 teaspoon soy sauce

1 package mizuna (or other tender green leaf lettuce), about 4 ounces (110 g)

Cut the pork into bite-sized slices. Heat the olive oil in a large frying pan. Add the pork and sauté on medium heat until cooked through. Add the pickled plums and continue to cook, using a wooden spoon to pull apart the flesh of the plums. Add the sugar and soy sauce, and mix well. Cut the mizuna into 2-inch (5 cm) lengths and arrange on a plate. Arrange the pork slices on top, and serve.

Riesling
Gewürztraminer

To pair this with white may not be surprising, pork being a white meat. Not so obvious is that a halbtrocken Riesling can transform the dish. The saltiness and the acidity of the plum make the wine taste milder and fruitier, while the pronounced sweet fruitiness of the wine with its own additional acidity enhances the pork in much the same way that Europeans traditionally use the acidity and fruit in apple sauce to enhance simple roast pork. Perhaps a more "nouvelle" approach would be a Californian Gewürztraminer with its more exotic flavor profile. More often than not this variety has a little residual sugar to round out its characteristic spicy finish, which makes it suitable for this dish, but better make sure that this is the case with your selected wine.

White wine pairs well with pork, and the fattier the pork the richer the wine should be. The cut required for this dish is quite fatty, so a medium to full-bodied, barrel-aged Chardonnay from a warmer climate such as California would be ideal. The barrel aging contributes a vanilla characteristic on the palate that will complement the sweetness of the white beans and pork fat. A soft, ripe, fruity Merlot from California will have these same characteristics. A quick hint: a drop of Tabasco in a dish such as this will spin it in favor of red.

SLOW-COOKED WHITE BEANS AND PORK

SERVES 6

2 cups dried white beans	2 medium onions, diced
1 pound (450 g) belly pork	3 1/4 cups water
4 tablespoons olive oil	2 1/2 bouillon cubes
3 cloves garlic, minced	dash sugar
3 medium tomatoes, diced	salt and pepper to taste

Soak the white beans for half a day or overnight, then rinse and drain, and set aside. Cut the pork into 1-inch (2 1/2 cm) cubes. Heat 1 tablespoon olive oil in a large saucepan. Add the garlic and sauté to release the flavor. Add all the remaining ingredients to the saucepan and cover. Simmer on low heat until the beans are soft.

An enamel saucepan will ensure that the pork becomes very tender and flavorful.

OVEN-BAKED SPARERIBS WITH VEGETABLES

SERVES 6

MARINADE

6 tablespoons soy sauce

6 tablespoons mirin

4 tablespoons sugar

5 cloves garlic, cut in half
   lengthwise

1 pound 5 1/2 ounces (600 g) pork
   spareribs

7 ounces (200 g) kabocha squash

10 stalks asparagus

10 pearl onions

10 button mushrooms

20 baby carrots

Preheat the oven to 350°F (180°C). Combine the soy sauce, mirin, and sugar in a small bowl, and mix well, then add the garlic. Place the spareribs in a large shallow dish and cover with marinade. Marinate for about 1 1/2 hours. Slice off some of the kabocha peel, and cut the kabocha into large bite-sized pieces. Cut the asparagus stalks in half. Remove the spareribs from the marinade and arrange on a cooking sheet. Cook in the oven for 15 minutes, then add the vegetables around them for another 15 to 25 minutes, basting with the marinade every few minutes to keep the meat moist and the vegetables flavorful. Arrange the spareribs and vegetables on a large serving dish. Drizzle with any remaining marinade, heated.

Malbec
Cabernet Sauvignon

Whether you use pork or substitute beef, you will need a wine with a solid core of ripe fruit plus enough body to cope with the fat and the strong flavors of the dish. Pork is a white meat, therefore you might think a lighter wine, such as Pinot, would suffice, but the quantity of soy sauce, mirin, and garlic prohibit this. The wine should have some tannin and acidity, and a Malbec from Argentina would seem to meet the bill, although a Cabernet Sauvignon from Australia also works. For the beef, try something a little more substantial, such as a Californian Cabernet from Napa Valley if you can afford it!

SAUTÉED PORK AND AVOCADO SAUCE

SERVES 4

4 thick slices pork shoulder,
   about 1 pound (450 g)

dash salt

dash black pepper

1 tablespoon olive oil

1 clove garlic, minced

1 ripe avocado

1 medium potato

8 pods fresh green peas

SAUCE

3 tablespoons water

1 tablespoon soy sauce

2 tablespoons mirin

1 tablespoon mayonnaise

1 tablespoon sugar

dash black pepper

Season the pork with salt and pepper to taste. Heat the olive oil in a frying pan, add the minced garlic, and sauté until fragrant. Add the pork slices and brown on both sides. Mince the avocado, and add it to the frying pan. Combine the water, soy sauce, mirin, mayonnaise, sugar and pepper in a bowl, then add to the frying pan. Cook uncovered for 2 to 3 minutes on medium, until the sauce thickens. Place the potato (in its skin) in a microwave-safe dish, cover, and microwave for 5 minutes. Drop the green peas into boiling salted water and boil for 3 to 4 minutes. Arrange the pork on a serving plate, and spoon the sauce over it. Remove the skin from the potato and slice. Arrange the potato and peapods around the meat.

❙ This recipe also works very well with beef or chicken.

Chardonnay
Pinot Noir

Despite the fact that pork is a white meat, it tends to have a lot of fat, which is quite sweet. As it is here fried with mayonnaise and avocado to create a really creamy texture, it can partner equally well with a full-bodied, barrel-aged Chardonnay or a ripe, fruity Pinot Noir from New Zealand or California. The latter goes well as avocado also leans towards red, especially when combined with soy sauce, while the weight and richness of barrel-aged Chardonnay will match up to that of the dish. A quick tip: if you are uncertain about the Chardonnay, look for about 14% alcohol on the label, as this will put you in the ballpark for a full-bodied wine.

STEAMED PORK AND CABBAGE WITH YUZU

SERVES 4

5 cabbage leaves

8 ounces (220 g) thin-sliced belly pork

peel of 1 yuzu, grated

SAUCE

3 tablespoons soy sauce

2 teaspoons vinegar

Spread one cabbage leaf over the bottom of a steamer and place two or three slices of pork on top of this, and some grated yuzu peel over that. Following the same order, layer the rest of the cabbage, pork, and yuzu peel in the steamer. Cover and steam for 10 minutes on high heat, then remove and arrange on a serving plate. Combine the soy sauce and vinegar, and pour over the cabbage and pork.

A simple way to prepare this dish is to layer the cabbage, pork, and yuzu in a microwave-safe container, cover, and microwave for 3 to 4 minutes.

Riesling
Sauvignon Blanc

The selection of fatty pork with cooked cabbage gives the dish sweetness, yet because the pork is steamed and combined with citrus, the dish is still light and elegant. This sweetness matches well with a halbtrocken German Riesling, while the fresh citrus characteristics of both food and wine complement each other. The parameters are white, aromatic, with no oak, and with slight residual sugar. Sauvignon Blanc is an obvious alternative, with its fresh, clean, flavors. A quick tip: vinegar and wine tend to jar, so try replacing the vinegar with yuzu juice for a milder sauce with a more citrus character, which makes an excellent counterpoint to the wine.

PORK AND OYSTER ROLL

SERVES 4

8 slices thin-sliced pork, about 8 ounces (220 g)

8 fresh oysters

1 tablespoon olive oil

dash salt

dash pepper

rucola leaves

2 limes, cut into wedges

Lay the slices of pork out on a cutting board and pound them with a meat pounder to tenderize them. Place one oyster at the edge of a slice of pork, roll, and secure with a toothpick. Repeat for all the oysters and slices of pork. Heat the olive oil in a frying pan, add the pork and oyster rolls, and sauté until well browned. Season with salt and pepper to taste. Arrange on a bed of rucola and garnish with lime wedges.

Champagne
Grüner Veltliner

While the flavors of the pork and the oysters are pronounced, they are still easily overpowered. It is interesting to contrast the food with and without lime, or alternatively sudachi juice, when matching with wine. Champagne works with or without. On the one hand it enhances the individual components of the dish, specifically the mineral character of the oysters. On the other hand, add the lime and everything combines with a fresher overtone. A Grüner Veltliner from Austria matches the weight of the pork, yet interestingly, with the addition of sudachi the oyster flavor is highlighted. Basically, you are looking for a white with good weight, slightly neutral, with little or no oak aging. An Albariño from Rías Baixas in Spain also holds possibilities.

YAKITORI

SERVES 4

SAUCE

6 tablespoons soy sauce

6 tablespoons mirin

1 tablespoon sugar

2 tablespoons water

1 pound (450 g) chicken thigh meat (boneless)

1 tablespoon olive oil

shichimi seven-spice pepper (or chili pepper), to taste

shishitō peppers

To make the sauce, combine the soy sauce, mirin, sugar, and water in a frying pan, and simmer on low heat until the mixture is reduced by about 10%. Set aside. Cut the chicken into bite-sized pieces. Add the olive oil to a large iron skillet, spread it over the bottom of the pan with a paper towel, and heat until the oil just begins to smoke. Add the chicken pieces and cook them, turning several times, until they are golden brown on both sides. Thread them onto bamboo skewers, brush with sauce, then return to the skillet, and heat again to set the flavor. Arrange the chicken skewers on a serving plate, drizzle with sauce, and sprinkle with shichimi to taste. Sear the shishitō peppers in the same skillet, and serve with the yakitori.

A tasty alternative is to season the chicken liberally with salt and pepper before cooking instead of brushing with sauce. While cooking, sprinkle occasionally with an extra dash of salt. Salt-flavored yakitori is best served with shichimi seven-spice red pepper and drizzled with lemon juice.

❙ If bamboo skewers are not available, metal ones may be used.

Gavi
Chianti

In the case of the plain, salted yakitori, the white meat, together with the simplicity of preparation and ingredients, invites a host of possible matches. Traditionally chargrilled, the key would be white wines with delicate fruit flavors and aromas: a Gavi from Italy or a simple white Bordeaux are good examples. Chargrilled, the fat drips off, but if pan-fried, as here, slightly more full-bodied wines are required, so look to the south of France, such as Coteaux de l'Ardéche. With the addition of the sauce, the selection changes in favor of a light red. Try a simple Chianti, like those in the traditional "fiasco" straw-wrapped bottles. If you wish to mix and match the yakitori, try a Beaujolais (especially Nouveau, released yearly on the third Thursday of November) with its fresh fruity flavors and subtle tannins.

WASABI-FLAVORED CHICKEN

SERVES 6

8 ounces (220 g) chicken breasts or
thighs (boneless)

1 bunch watercress, about 4 ounces
(110 g)

SAUCE

1 tablespoon soy sauce

1 tablespoon mirin

1 teaspoon wasabi

Boil the chicken pieces for 15 to 18 minutes. Drain and allow to cool,
then shred finely by hand, and place in a large bowl. Cut the watercress into 1-inch (2½ cm) lengths, boil for 3 to 4 minutes, drain, and
mix with the chicken. Combine the soy sauce, mirin, and wasabi in a
small bowl, then add to the chicken and watercress, and toss well.

Sancerre
Muscadet

"White meat, white wine" rings
true in this case, as the mild flavors of the dish support a light to
medium-bodied fresh fruity wine
with a lively acidity. If you show
restraint with the wasabi, Sancerre
from the Loire is just the ticket.
It's a dry white, with crisp acidity, and marked Sauvignon flavors of gooseberries, citric fruits,
or currant leaves that, in this
case, match the watercress to
perfection, as well as adding
freshness. A good alternative is a
young Muscadet from the same
region. Look for "sur lie" on the
bottle, since they have an extra
complexity from being aged on
their lees for an extended period
(the lees being the sediment of
dead yeasts that accumulates at
the bottom of the barrel after
fermentation). This gives the
wine more flavor, fruit, and often
a slight spritziness, which further
lifts the fruit. Both are best consumed young, so look for the
youngest vintage.

JAPANESE-STYLE CHICKEN LOAF

SERVES 6

- 1 naganegi (or leek), about 11 ounces (300 g), minced
- 2 bouillon cubes
- 1 pound (450 g) ground chicken
- 2 carrots, grated
- ⅓ cup (80 g) bread crumbs
- 2 eggs
- dash salt
- dash pepper
- baby leaf greens
- 1 jar white asparagus, about 6 stalks

Place the naganegi in a microwave-safe dish, cover, and microwave for 2 minutes. Crumble the bouillon cubes into a mixing bowl. Add the ground chicken, naganegi, carrots, bread crumbs, and eggs, and mix well. Sprinkle with salt and pepper to taste. Place the mixture in a small baking mold. Heat the oven to 350°F (180°C) and bake, uncovered, for 20 minutes. Transfer to a serving dish and slice. Serve with the baby leaf greens and white asparagus.

Chardonnay
Vouvray demi-sec

A full-bodied barrel-aged Chardonnay from a warm climate matches the dish weight-wise and interlocks perfectly. However, the union does tend to make them both seem heavy. Rather than a matching based on weight, then, look for a wine with balanced acidity and individual personality. My wild card was an old Vouvray demi-sec from the Loire. Made from Chenin Blanc, with age it had lost most of its sweetness yet still retained much of its personality and acidity. Needless to say, a sparkler such as a trocken sekt will lift the dish perfectly. The Riesling variety contributes its character, while the bubbles work their magic. Check for "Sekt b.a." on the label to ensure the quality.

CHICKEN AND CARROT SALAD

SERVES 4

1 pound (450 g) chicken breast

3 large carrots

dash salt

2 tablespoons vinegar

2 tablespoons sugar

1 tablespoon olive oil

1 sprig fresh dill for garnish

DRESSING

2 tablespoons mayonnaise

2 tablespoons mirin

1 tablespoon sugar

1 tablespoon vinegar

1 tablespoon olive oil

Boil the chicken for an hour, then drain and allow to cool. Cut the carrots into long matchsticks and place them in a small mixing bowl. Sprinkle them with salt, then mix the salt through them by hand, and set aside for a few minutes to soften. Add the vinegar, sugar, and olive oil to the carrots, and allow them to marinate for 30 minutes. Shred the chicken by hand and arrange it with the carrots on a serving plate. Combine the mayonnaise, mirin, sugar, vinegar, and olive oil in a small bowl, and whip until smooth. Just before eating, drizzle the dressing over the chicken and the carrots, and garnish with the sprig of dill.

The mayonnaise and mirin give the dressing a mild flavor and smooth texture. The marinated carrots are also good eaten by themselves.

Oeil-de-Perdrix
Soave

There is a saying that the Japanese eat with their eyes, and the Chinese with their stomachs. For the former, then, I would recommend Oeil-de-Perdrix, a dry, fresh, fruity rosé from Switzerland that creates visual harmony with the carrots and works wonders for this dish. Despite the subtle nature of the chicken, in combination with the ingredients this dish has mild, but pronounced flavors. Rosé with just a little tannin from the grape skins, which also contribute to its color, facilitates this nicely. The key here is a current vintage to guarantee the fresh fruitiness that will complement the dish. Alternatively, as this dish is relatively mild, Soave from Italy, a traditional favorite with chicken, should partner well.

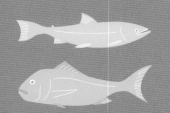

FISH AND SEAFOOD

PAN-FRIED SALMON WITH LEMON, SOY SAUCE, AND THYME

SERVES 8

salmon fillets, about 1 pound
   11 ounces (750 g)

salt to taste

1 lemon

sprigs of fresh thyme, to taste

DRESSING

2 tablespoons soy sauce

2 tablespoons olive oil

½ tablespoon sugar

juice of 1 lemon

Sprinkle the salmon with a small amount of salt and squeeze the juice of 1 lemon over the entire length of the fillets. Oil a medium-sized frying pan and place it on a medium-high flame to heat. Add the salmon and cook uncovered until almost completely heated through, then reduce the heat. Cut the other lemon in half, place both halves face-down in the frying pan with the salmon, and heat briefly to release the flavor. Remove and set aside. Add the thyme to the same pan and press to release the flavor. Remove and set aside. In a small bowl, combine the soy sauce, olive oil, sugar, and lemon juice, and mix to make the dressing. When the salmon is cooked, arrange the fillets on a platter with the heated lemon pieces, and drizzle with the dressing. Sprinkle with small pieces of the fragrant thyme.

Burgundy White
Pinot Noir

Acidity from lemon is best matched with a white wine with good acidity. Being from a cool climate, Champagne has a good acidity that matches well with the dish. Good white Burgundy with acidity mingles with the lemon. However, avoid Chardonnay from warmer climates as it has low acidity and lots of oak, making the wine too dominant on the palate. Alternatively, fatty salmon usually goes well with lighter reds from warmer climates. Though the acidity in these wines is not high, the acidity of lemon can add a certain dimension to the wine, so my choice in this case was a Pinot Noir from Santa Barbara.

TOFU AND SALMON STUFFED PEPPERS

SERVES 6

1 yellow bell pepper

1 red bell pepper

1 green bell pepper

1 package tofu, about 11 ounces (300 g)

fresh salmon fillets, about 5 1/2 ounces (150 g)

1 tablespoon butter

1/2 medium onion, minced

salt to taste

1 tablespoon soy sauce

1 teaspoon sugar

1 tablespoon potato starch (or cornstarch)

2 tablespoons olive oil

DRESSING

1 2/3 tablespoons (25 cc) soy sauce

1 2/3 tablespoons (25 cc) mirin

1 1/3 tablespoons (20 cc) water

1/2 tablespoon sugar

1 teaspoon potato starch (or cornstarch)

Cut all the peppers in half lengthwise and remove the core and seeds. Place in a microwave-safe dish, cover, and heat for 5 minutes in the microwave. Remove, place under cold running water, and remove the skin. Wrap the tofu in a paper towel and squeeze out as much moisture as possible, and then place with the salmon in a food processor, and mix. Melt the butter in a small saucepan, then add the onion and sauté until softened. Combine the tofu and salmon mixture and onion in a small bowl and mix well. Add the salt, soy sauce, sugar, and potato starch, and mix again. Place 2 tablespoons of the mixture onto each half pepper and form into a mound. Heat the olive oil briefly in a large saucepan on medium heat, and add the stuffed peppers, face-down so that the mixture will cook through. In a separate small saucepan, combine the ingredients for the dressing, mix, and simmer uncovered for 5 to 6 minutes on low heat. Arrange the peppers on a platter, drizzle with the dressing, and serve.

Koshu

German White

There are two types of tofu, momen (cotton) and kinu (silken). The latter in this case creates a soft, creamy texture similar to a mousse, while underlining the texture of the flavors of the peppers. The yellow pepper, sauce, and tofu all combine to contribute sweetness. Slightly sweet Koshu is the ideal match here, matching the sweetness of the dish while the delicate flavors of both harmonize. Otherwise use a white, light- to medium-bodied wine with some sweetness, but avoid dry wines with a high acidity. For example, a Müller-Thurgau from Germany pairs well, but look for Kabinett grade on the label. Avoid Riesling, as the characteristic acidity of the variety would clash.

SALMON MARINATED IN SAKÉ

SERVES 6

fresh salmon fillets, about 5 1/2 ounces
  (150 g)

1/2 teaspoon salt

ground roasted sesame seeds, to taste

1 shallot, minced

juice of 1 lemon

2 tablespoons olive oil

2 1/3 tablespoons sugar

5 tablespoons (60 cc) saké

fresh dill, to taste

1 sprig dill blossoms,
  for garnish

Slice the salmon paper-thin, and arrange on a platter. Sprinkle lightly with the salt and ground sesame seeds. Put the shallot, lemon juice, olive oil, sugar, and saké in a small bowl and mix well. Drizzle the mixture over the salmon. Sprinkle with fresh dill and garnish with small sprigs of dill blossoms.

Chardonnay Sparkling Wine

While the lemon eliminates the fishy character, the combination of sugar counterbalances the acidity of the lemon, leaving the dish on the sweeter side. Ideally, the saké in the dish makes saké the perfect counterpoint, especially if you purchase it fresh for the occasion. Otherwise, the salmon needs a wine with some character. An Australian Chardonnay works well, though the dish requires one with a little residual sugar and perhaps a hint of toastiness from oak to balance the character of the fish. Needless to say, a Brut sparkling wine works its magic: my choice is an Italian Oltrepò Pavese DOC, a rosé made from Pinot Nero.

AROMATIC BAKED SALMON

SERVES 4

4 salmon fillets, about 1 pound
  (450 g)

4 hajikami pickled ginger
  shoots

MARINADE

3 tablespoons soy sauce

2 tablespoons saké

5 tablespoons mirin

peel of 1 yuzu, grated

Place the salmon fillets in a casserole or other wide shallow dish. In a small bowl, combine the ingredients for the marinade and mix well. Pour over the salmon slices, and marinate for 4 to 5 hours. Preheat the oven to 350°F (180°C) and cook the marinated salmon for 10 minutes, until golden brown. Serve each fillet with a shoot of hajikami pickled ginger.

Sauvignon Blanc Champagne

With the very first bite, the aroma of the yuzu rind prevails. What the dish calls for is a white, non-oaked, aromatic wine, so my initial choice would be a dry but riper style Sauvignon Blanc, such as those from the Marlborough region, as we are not looking for too much acidity. Serious Sauvignon can go tête-à-tête with the yuzu, forming a dynamic combination. Alternatively, vintage Champagne is the connoisseur's choice. Age rounds out acidity and increases the effect of umami, while also developing soy characteristics, and seems to go hand in hand with this dish.

SIMMERED FISH

Sweet Simmered Herring

SERVES 4

2 herring fillets, about 8 ounces (220 g)

1 tablespoon olive oil

2 tablespoons mirin

1 1/2 tablespoons sugar

3 tablespoons soy sauce

Cut each fillet in half to make four pieces. Heat the olive oil in a medium-sized saucepan. Add the herring, cover, and sauté on medium heat, turning once, until both sides are golden brown. Add the mirin, sugar, and soy sauce, and simmer on low heat until the liquid is completely absorbed.

Sardines with Saké and Umeboshi

SERVES 4

3 small sardines, about 1 pound

1 cup water

2 umeboshi pickled plums

2 tablespoons saké

1 tablespoon soy sauce

1 tablespoon sugar

Prepare the sardines by removing the entrails (see page 115); rinse the sardines well and pat dry. Place the water and the umeboshi in a medium-sized saucepan, add the saké, soy sauce, and sugar, then cover and simmer on low heat for about 15 minutes, until the liquid is reduced by one-third. Place the fish in a microwave-safe dish, add the umeboshi and liquid, cover and cook in the microwave for 3 to 4 minutes.

Simmered Flounder

SERVES 2

1 cup water	2 tablespoons saké
3 thin slices fresh ginger	2 tablespoons mirin
3 tablespoons soy sauce	1 flounder, about 7 ounces (200 g)

Place the water and the sliced ginger in a medium saucepan, add the soy sauce, saké, mirin, and lastly the flounder with the skin side up. Cover and simmer on low for about 15 minutes, until the liquid is reduced by one-third. To prepare this dish in a microwave oven, put all ingredients together in a microwave-safe dish and cook for 2 to 3 minutes.

Lambrusco
Red Vinho Verde
Provence Rosé

Fresh herring is an oily fish, and combined with soy sauce and sugar it loses its fishiness. The wine therefore has to be red, fruity, with a little residual sugar. A red Lambrusco works well, and served cold the *frizzante* and temperature freshens the palate. The key word on the label is secco (dry, though still with 10 g/l). Another choice might be a sparkling Shiraz from Australia. • Sardine is oily. In Portugal, grilled sardines are traditionally served with a red Vinho Verde, which has a good acidity and a slight spritz. Combined with sugar, soy sauce, and mirin, some residual sugar is needed. With good acidity and a slight spritziness designed to accentuate the aromas, Roero Arneis can freshen the palate by cutting the oil, while the aromatic components add an additional dimension. • Flat fish calls for white wine. However with soy sauce, which the top layer of the fish absorbs, try a dry fruity rosé from Provence. A Sauvignon also works well with the ginger influence.

SILVER COD SIMMERED IN SPICY MISO

SERVES 4

1 cup water

4 or 5 slices fresh ginger

1 clove garlic, minced

2 tablespoons sugar

2 tablespoons soy sauce

4 teaspoons miso

2 tablespoons kochijan spicy miso

silver cod fillet, about 5 ½ ounces (150 g)

chili pepper to taste

Place the water, ginger, garlic, sugar, soy sauce, miso, and kochijan in a medium-sized saucepan and bring to a boil. Add the fillet, cover, and simmer on low heat for ten minutes, or until the liquid is reduced by about half. Arrange on a serving platter, sprinkle with chili pepper, and serve.

Sparkling Red
Pinot Noir

An oily fish combined with an aromatic and fragrant sauce, with strong ingredients that are both spicy and sweet, requires a red fruit-driven wine, preferably one with a little residual sugar to compete. My choice of preference was a sparkling red, which has a strong character and flavor, plus some residual sugar. The versatile fizz allows the wine to interlock and complement the dish harmoniously. A warm climate Pinot Noir with its ripe forward fruit also works well. Avoid cool climate Pinots, especially Burgundy, as the understated elegance of these wines would be overpowered.

TOMATO SLICES TOPPED WITH SCALLOPS AND ANCHOVIES

SERVES 8

1 tablespoon butter

8 scallops

2 tomatoes

1 anchovy fillet

2 tablespoons tonburi (or caviar)

Heat the butter in a medium-sized frying pan and add the scallops. Heat through, turning once, until both sides are golden brown. Remove and set aside. Cut the tomatoes into ½-inch (1 cm) slices (you will need eight slices in total) and arrange these on a platter. Place one scallop on top of each tomato slice. Cut the anchovy fillet into 8 pieces, and place one piece on top of each scallop. Pile the tonburi on top of each appetizer.

Champagne
Chardonnay

While the scallops are the focal point, the tonburi contributes a crunchy texture and the tomato gives a nice amount of acidity to balance the buttery flavors of the scallop. Brut Champagne from an older vintage interacts harmoniously with the individual ingredients, allowing each to prevail. Alternatively, a medium-bodied Chardonnay that has undergone malolactic fermentation will illustrate how similar textures can unite to create a synergy. Apart from smoothing the mouth feel, the latter technique results in a by-product called diacetyl, which can impart an attractive, almost buttery character to the wine. If you substitute tonburi with caviar, however, stick with the Champagne.

STEAMED SCALLOPS

SERVES 5

5 scallops

1 tablespoon garlic, finely minced

1 tablespoon fresh ginger, finely minced

1 tablespoon onion, finely minced

1 tablespoon green onion, finely minced

dash sugar

dash nampla fish sauce

dash soy sauce

chives, for garnish

Place the scallops in a medium-sized saucepan. Sprinkle with the garlic, ginger, onion, and green onion, and then add the sugar, nampla, and soy sauce. Cover and steam for 10 minutes. Arrange the scallops on a platter and drizzle with any remaining liquid from the pan. Garnish with the chives.

Chardonnay
Champagne

This dish is tricky. However, experience has proven that grilled scallops and Corton Charlemagne are sublime. It still works in this case, although you need to go easy on the garlic and ginger as they tend to kill the flavor of the wine. Basically you need a full-bodied white with a balanced acidity. Chardonnay from around the world will work as long as it is from a cooler climate area, and ideally with a couple of years of bottle aging. If you do not want to take a risk, Brut Champagne is without doubt the primary choice.

THIN-SLICED OCTOPUS WITH SUDACHI DIP

SERVES 6

1 large octopus tentacle, about 12 1/2 ounces (350 g), boiled

1 sudachi citrus, halved, for garnish (optional)

chives, for garnish

DIPPING SAUCE

1 1/2 tablespoons soy sauce

1 tablespoon vinegar

1/2 tablespoon mirin

1 teaspoon yuzu pepper paste

juice of 1 sudachi citrus

Slice the octopus as thinly as possible, and arrange on a serving plate. Garnish with sudachi halves and chives. Combine the soy sauce, vinegar, mirin, yuzu pepper paste and sudachi juice, and serve in a small bowl as a dipping sauce for the octopus.

Gruner Veltliner
Champagne

The inherent spicy quality of a Grüner Veltliner from Austria not only matches the refreshing yuzu pepper paste, but additionally has the weight and structure to create a more complex taste. What you need to avoid with this dish are wines with a dominant character, oak aging, and residual sugar. There are different types of umami, and when alternatives are united they enhance the savory effect. Umami is found in Champagne due to the contact with the lees during the second fermentation. Combining this with the umami inherent in octopus and soy sauce, therefore, creates a synergy enhancing the savory component and adding freshness through acidity, bubbles, and serving temperature.

DEEP-FRIED OCTOPUS WITH EDAMAME

SERVES 6

1 large octopus tentacle, about 12 ½
   ounces (350 g)

¼ cup potato starch (or cornstarch)

vegetable oil (for deep-frying)

⅓ cup dried thin-sliced konbu

½ cup edamame, boiled and shelled

SAUCE

2 tablespoons dashi stock (see
   page 114)

2 tablespoons soy sauce

1 tablespoon mirin

½ tablespoon sugar

Cut the octopus meat into bite-sized pieces, and coat well with potato starch. Heat the oil in a wok or large frying pan, and deep-fry the octopus meat until it is lightly browned. Remove from the oil with a slotted spoon and drain well. Deep-fry the konbu in the same pan until it is crisp, remove and drain on paper towels. Put the dashi, soy sauce, mirin and sugar in a small saucepan, bring to a boil, and remove from heat. Spread the deep-fried konbu out on a serving plate and arrange the octopus on top. Sprinkle with edamame and drizzle with the sauce.

Champagne
Dry Rosé

As the octopus is deep-fried, Champagne would be the drink of choice. Champagne typically has a higher acidity then other sparkling wines, and this helps cut through any greasiness. The bubbles contribute to a refreshing mouth feel, and at the same time accentuate the character of the dish. Given the ingredients and style of cooking, a fresh aromatic rosé would be your next best choice. Look to the South of France, such as a Coteaux d'Aix en Provence from a current vintage.

As with all crustaceans, crab traditionally pairs with lighter whites. However, here combined with the sweetness from the cooked naganegi and mixed with mayonnaise and fresh cream, it requires a medium- to full-bodied white. A premium oak-aged Chardonnay that has undergone malolactic fermentation and battonage (stirring of lees), from a cool climate, such as New Zealand, matches well. The latter vinification techniques create a softer, fuller wine with a rounded acidity that counterbalances the ingredients of the dish. Alternatively, try a Chardonnay from Burgundy, the key here being to have Premier Cru or Grand Cru on the label and a good vintage. The full, rounded character of a vintage Champagne partners the naganegi, while cutting through the oil in the mayonnaise to create perfection.

NAGANEGI STUFFED WITH CRABMEAT

SERVES 6

2 thick naganegi (or leeks)	1 tablespoon mayonnaise
$5/6$ cup (200 cc) water	dash sugar
1 teaspoon gelatin	3 $1/2$ ounces (100 g) crabmeat,
$1/2$ chicken bouillon cube	cooked and shredded
2 tablespoons fresh cream	

Cut the naganegi into 1 $1/2$ inch (4 cm) lengths, and add to a saucepan of boiling water for 6 to 7 minutes, until they are slightly soft. Drain and cool. When cool, push out and remove the centers, leaving only about 2 layers of skin. Combine the water, gelatin, and bouillon cube in a small microwave-safe bowl, cover, and microwave for 1 minute. Take out 2 $2/3$ tablespoons (40 cc) of the gelatin liquid and place it in a separate small mixing bowl, add the fresh cream, mayonnaise, sugar, and crabmeat, and mix. Set this bowl into a larger bowl of ice to chill. When the mixture has jelled, use it to stuff the naganegi pieces. Refrigerate the remaining gelatin mixture for about 2 hours. When chilled, spread it over a serving plate, and arrange the stuffed naganegi on top.

SHRIMP SAUTÉED WITH LEMONGRASS

SERVES 4

20 fresh, medium-sized shrimp

2 tablespoons olive oil

2 cloves garlic, minced

¼ sprig lemongrass, minced

2 tablespoons sugar

1 tablespoon soy sauce

1 teaspoon nampla fish sauce

Shell and devein the shrimp. Heat the olive oil in a large frying pan, add the garlic and lemongrass, and heat until fragrant. Add the shrimp and continue to heat, stirring, until they whiten and curl. Combine the sugar, soy sauce, and nampla in a small bowl, and add to the pan. Continue to heat, stirring, until the liquid is absorbed.

For an interesting variation on this recipe, substitute the shrimp with 5 scallops, each cut into 2 discs, and use just 1 tablespoon olive oil for frying.

Sparkling Red
Roero Arneis

The tannins in sparkling red wine are accentuated by the bubbles and serving temperature, so the trick to making sparkling reds is in balancing the residual sugar to smooth out these otherwise bitter tannins. Soy sauce, sugar, and garlic create a formidable combination that requires a red wine. However, a chilled sparkling red not only counterbalances the ingredients of the sauce, but instills freshness due to the serving temperature. In addition to this freshness, the bubbles accentuate the lemongrass character. Similarly, aromatic whites typically inherit bitterness from the skin, so the winemaker's trick is the same. Varieties like Roero Arneis will work equally well, the residual sugar acting as a counterpoint while the aromatic nature lifts the dish.

Though crustaceans require white wine, this dish still offers great latitude. Either sparkling wine, Champagne, or a full-bodied white will work like magic. The inherent saltiness in the lobster requires a full-bodied white with subtle fruit flavors that can also come to terms with the savory sauce, to create a balance. If you go with Chardonnay, try to pick one with a good acidity and a minimal amount of oak from a cooler region such as Carneros in California. The acidity will balance out the vinegar, and although some oak will lend complexity, too much will distort the flavor of the lobster. An interesting alternative is trocken Grauburgunder from Germany. In this case, the inherent spicy character of the variety blends well with the chives while adding complexity to the dish.

LOBSTER DIP

SERVES 4

1 whole lobster

DIPPING SAUCE
2 tablespoons minced chives
1 tablespoon vinegar
2 tablespoons soy sauce

Place the lobster in a large saucepan of boiling water, cover, and boil for 7 to 8 minutes, or until the lobster turns red. Remove and leave to cool. Pull off the head and tail, and use scissors to remove the meat from the body. Arrange the lobster on a serving plate. Combine the chives, vinegar, and soy sauce, and then divide between four small bowls as a dipping sauce for the lobster.

In Japan, Ise ebi, or Japanese spiny lobster, is often used, as in the photo.

SEAFOOD WITH CARROT DRESSING

SERVES 8

10 amaebi sweet shrimp

10 mussels

1 whole squid, about 5 ¹/₂ ounces
(150 g) (see page 116)

3 ounces (80 g) fillet of salmon

3 ounces (80 g) fillet of tuna

2 scallops

1 okra

DRESSING

¹/₂ cup grated carrot

¹/₃ cup vinegar

¹/₃ cup soy sauce

3 tablespoons sugar

Shell and devein the amaebi. Clean the mussels and boil until they open; discard the shells. Cut the amaebi, squid, salmon, tuna, and scallops into half-inch, bite-sized pieces. Thinly slice the okra. Arrange the seafood on a serving plate and scatter the okra slices over the top. Just before serving, combine the carrot, vinegar, soy sauce and sugar in a small bowl, and drizzle over the seafood.

> It is essential to use only the freshest ingredients, as they are served uncooked.

Sparkling Wine
Graves White

While the vinegar in the dressing gives a refreshing touch, it does require a wine with character. In addition, the sauce is also quite prominent and on the sweeter side. All this combined with an assortment of fish is best paired with the versatile fizz. Ideally, take one from a warmer climate, where the focus is on fruit rather than on acidity. Try Southern Australia. Alternatively, from Bordeaux a Graves white, though from a minor chateau to avoid the use of too much new oak. This is typically a blend of Sauvignon and Semillon, in which case look for those that have a higher percentage of Semillon so that the strong Sauvignon character doesn't dominate the dish.

OYSTERS ON THE HALF SHELL WITH JAPANESE DRESSING

SERVES 3

3 oysters (in the shell)
1 slice daikon radish, about 2 inches (5 cm)
3 small fresh red chili peppers
dash soy sauce
3 slices of lime

Remove half of the shell of each oyster, place the half shells containing the oysters on ice to chill. Next, use a chopstick to make three holes through the daikon slice, and insert one red chili pepper into each. Grate so that both daikon and chili peppers are grated together. Place one third of the mixture on each oyster. Add a dash of soy sauce and a slice of lime to each, and serve.

Chablis
Pomerol

The classic companion for oysters is the crisp, slightly neutral, white Muscadet from the Loire. However, the addition of soy sauce, daikon radish, and red chili pepper calls for something more substantial, such as Chablis Premier Cru or Champagne. If you are interested in experimenting, note that oysters have a great deal of umami of a type that reacts negatively to tannin in young red wines. Nevertheless, an old Pomerol from Bordeaux works. Pomerols tend to be the least tannic of Bordeaux wines, and with age the tannins from the oak will have rounded out and precipitated.

JELLIED VEGETABLES AND SEAFOOD

SERVES 8

1 medium zucchini

¹/₄ yellow bell pepper

¹/₄ orange bell pepper

¹/₄ red bell pepper

1 okra

10 small shrimp

JELLY

2 cups dashi stock (see page 114)

2 teaspoons gelatin

2 teaspoons soy sauce

1 teaspoon mirin

dash salt

Chop the zucchini and all the bell peppers into roughly ¹/₄-inch (¹/₂ cm) pieces and drop into boiling water for 2 to 3 minutes, then drain. Slice the okra. Boil the shrimp in their shells. When the shrimps curl, remove from the water, drain, and cool. Shell and devein, and cut into ¹/₂-inch (1 cm) pieces. To make the jelly, combine the dashi and gelatin in a small saucepan over low heat, stirring to dissolve the gelatin. Add the soy sauce, mirin, and salt, bring to a boil, and simmer for 2 to 3 minutes. Remove from the heat and cool. Place the jelly, all the vegetables, and the shrimp together into a mold, mix well, and chill in the refrigerator for 3 to 4 hours until set.

Sauvignon Blanc
Sparkling Wine

Shrimp without a strong sauce pairs with white wine. This dish has quite delicate integrated flavors, especially as the summer vegetables are diced, so a white wine is called for. The summer wine par excellence is a New Zealand Sauvignon Blanc. Not only do these vibrant, fruit-driven wines create a foil for the dish, but inherent in their aromas and flavors are some of the characters of the vegetables. As a summer starter, I would serve this dish with a soft, round sparkler, the bubble creating an extra textural dimension.

STEAMED MUSSELS WITH BUTTER, GARLIC, AND SAKÉ

SERVES 8

1 tablespoon butter	1 cup saké
2 cloves garlic, minced	1 tablespoon soy sauce
1 pound (450 g) mussels	1 tablespoon minced chives

Heat the butter in a saucepan, add the minced garlic, and sauté until fragrant. Add the mussels and the saké, then cover the pan and continue cooking until the mussels open. Drizzle the soy sauce over all while moving the pan from side to side. Transfer to a serving plate and sprinkle with the minced chives.

Champagne
Sauvignon Blanc

Wonderful as a starter accompanied by a glass of Champagne!
Alternatively, a Sauvignon
Blanc from New Zealand, with
its crisp, clean, full flavors, will
pair equally well. Since this is
typically fermented and aged in
stainless steel to preserve the fruit
character, there will be no con-
flict from oak. The refreshing,
nerve-tingling acidity deals well
with the butter, while the fresh,
forward, aromatic nose, typically
of gooseberries, cut grass, and
even civet, competes equally
with the garlic. For perfection,
add some of the wine of choice
to the dish while steaming (or
even wholly substitute the saké).

Champagne
Riesling Sekt

Sparkling wines work exceptionally well with deep fried foods in general, and this dish is no exception. Surprisingly, however, it is the burdock that seals the choice for Brut Champagne or a Riesling trocken sekt, since in this dish it has a slight sweetness. Both wines seem to spotlight this sweetness as a result of their acidity, while the serving temperature and bubbles freshen up the dish. Then again, a white wine from the South of France with a smooth mouth feel provides a perfect match weightwise, underlining the flavors of the snapper and salt, while the soft ripe fruit and mineral overtones broaden the overall profile.

DEEP-FRIED SEA BREAM WITH BURDOCK

SERVES 4

1 burdock root
1 sea bream, about 10 inches (25 cm) long
dash salt
⅓ cup flour
vegetable oil (for deep-frying)

The flavors of the sea bream and burdock are complementary, so it's best to combine both tastes in each bite.

Scrub the burdock well, and rinse. Cut it into 4-inch (10 cm) lengths, and then cut each of these into matchsticks, as finely as possible. Place the burdock in a bowl of cold water and soak for 10 minutes to remove the astringency. Scale the sea bream and prepare it in the san-mai oroshi style (see page 116), separating the meat from the bones, but leaving the head and tail connected to the main bone of the fish. Chop the meat into pieces about 1 inch (2 ½ cm) wide, sprinkle these with salt, and coat them well with flour. Heat the oil in a wok or large frying pan to 350°F (180°C). Deep-fry the sea bream pieces until they are lightly golden on both sides, then remove from the oil with a slotted spoon. Drain well. When cool, pat dry to remove any excess oil. Deep-fry the head, tail, and main bone for about 5 minutes. (Do not coat these pieces, they are used for presentation only.) Remove and drain well. Drain the burdock and pat it very dry. Place it in the oil and deep-fry for about 2 minutes until crispy. Arrange the head, bone, and tail on the plate as a base. Arrange the meat of the sea bream over the bone, and serve the crispy burdock on the side of the plate.

TUNA TATAKI WITH WASABI

SERVES 8

1 tablespoon vegetable oil

block of tuna, about 1 pound (450 g)

¼ cup spring onions, minced very finely

1 sprig flowering shiso, for garnish
   (optional)

DIPPING SAUCE

2 tablespoons soy sauce

1 teaspoon wasabi

Prepare a large bowl of cold water with ice cubes added. Use a paper towel to spread the oil over the surface of a stainless steel frying pan, and heat. Add the block of tuna and heat, turning several times, until all sides are seared. Remove the tuna from the heat and place it immediately in the iced water to prevent it from cooking further. When it is chilled, remove from the water, pat dry, and slice into ¼-inch (½-cm) slices. Arrange the slices of tuna in a ring on a serving plate, and mound the spring onions in the center of the ring. Garnish with the sprig of flowering shiso. Combine the soy sauce and wasabi in a small dish as a dipping sauce for the tuna slices.

Tinto de Toro (Tempranillo)
Pinot Noir

Beware! While tuna is tuna, some cuts are fattier than others. Living in Japan you become keenly aware of the three types: akami (red meat), chū-toro (medium fat) and ō-toro (the fattiest). If using fatty tuna, match your toro with a red from the Toro D.O. The strength and powerful flavors engendered by these Spanish reds made from Tinto de Toro (Tempranillo) can cope with the combination of fatty tuna, soy sauce, and wasabi. If you use a non-fatty akami cut and go easy on the wasabi, a lighter red such as a Pinot Noir will work perfectly, as will a full-bodied Chardonnay from a warmer region such as California.

RICE AND NOODLES

NIGIRIZUSHI

SERVES 6

9 cups of sushi rice (see page 113)

1 whole squid, about 5½ ounces (150 g) (see page 116)

1 jar pickled herring, about 5½ ounces (150 g)

5½ ounces (150 g) salmon fillet

5½ ounces (150 g) tuna fillet

6 medium shrimp

1 cucumber

2 tablespoons wasabi paste

4 tablespoons ikura salmon roe

Cut the squid and herring into pieces 1 inch (2½ cm) by 2 inches (5 cm). Cut the salmon and tuna into slices ¼ inch (½ cm) thick, 1 inch (2½ cm) wide and 2 inches (5 cm) long. Remove the head of the shrimp and the shell from around the body, but leave the tail attached. Thinly slice the cucumber on the diagonal. Take an egg-sized handful of the sushi rice and softly squeeze it to make a bed of rice for each topping. Spread a small amount of wasabi on each. Place a slice of squid, herring, salmon, or tuna, on top of each bed of rice. Place a slice of cucumber on a bed of rice and top this with a small amount of ikura.

▌ Make sure you use only the freshest fish, as it will be eaten uncooked.

Champagne

Three raw-fish sushi dishes are presented in this section—Nigiri-zushi, Scattered Seafood Sushi, and Bite-Sized Sushi Appetizers—and given the similarity between them, the advice for each is the same. While beer traditionally partners sushi, the dish can be savored happily in tandem with Champagne. The bubbles work just as well to scour and refresh the palate of fishy flavors, its versatility permitting one wine to match all. Otherwise you will need several wines to match the various fish.

Continued overleaf . . .

A medium-bodied white is required for the shellfish, while avocado by itself goes well with rosé. In the case of tuna, an akami cut harmonizes with a full-bodied Chardonnay from a warmer climate, while chū-toro leans toward red. Salmon also goes well with lighter reds such as Pinot. Ikura pairs with bubbles, although be sure to avoid fruity styles and focus on those from cooler climates. The addition of soy sauce and wasabi, however, can tip it all in favor of red. If the wasabi is fresh and the fish is dipped lightly in the soy sauce (rice should never be dipped in the soy sauce since it acts like a sponge), though, the fish may dictate your choice. In general, as sushi represents the fish in its purest form, look for wines that reflect the vine, not the vinivication process, so avoid wines that have been aged in oak. Likewise avoid those with tannins, especially if you choose red. Also keep in mind that in order to cut the fishy flavors, a certain amount of acidity is needed, which favors wine from cooler climates.

SCATTERED SEAFOOD SUSHI

SERVES 6

9 cups sushi rice (see page 113)

6 medium shrimp

3 1/2 ounces (100 g) fresh squid (see page 116)

3 1/2 ounces (100 g) tuna fillet

3 1/2 ounces (100 g) salmon fillet

3 fresh scallops

1 avocado

3 tablespoons ikura salmon roe

3 tablespoons wasabi paste

Boil the shrimp in their shells and then remove the shells. Roughly chop the squid, tuna, salmon, and scallops. Cut the avocado into 1/2-inch cubes. Mound the sushi rice into a serving bowl and top with the seafood, avocado, and wasabi.

SMOKED SALMON AND CUCUMBER
PRESSED SUSHI

SERVES 6

9 cups sushi rice (see page 113)
8 thin slices smoked salmon
    about 5½ ounces (150 g)

2 cucumbers
salt
3 tablespoons ikura salmon roe

Prepare a dish or mold approximately 8 inches (20 cm) square. Cut the smoked salmon into long thin strips the same width as the cucumbers, and the same length as the square mold. Cut the cucumbers to the same length as the mold, and then use a vegetable peeler to cut them into long, thin slices. Sprinkle a little salt on the cucumber slices to make them pliable. Place the sushi rice into the mold and press it down firmly. Place the cucumber strips along the top of the rice, and the salmon strips on top of these, and press down again lightly to make it flat (this will make it easier to cut the sushi later). Transfer the pressed sushi to a square serving plate, and mound the ikura on top, in the center.

VARIATION: Cut the smoked salmon into bite-sized pieces, and mix together with thinly sliced and salted cucumber. Add to the sushi rice and toss thoroughly. Arrange on a plate and sprinkle with white sesame seeds.

Brut Rosé Champagne
Champagne

Vinegar is normally regarded as the enemy of wine, yet it is a key ingredient in the sushi rice. Brut rosé Champagne tends to be slightly firmer or more robust than regular Champagne, and has just the right balance to cope and harmonize with it. With other wines, however, the flavor of the rice will either be obscured or seem sour. More importantly, the gentle flavors of the Champagne do not overpower those of the smoked salmon, forming symmetry. In addition, the slightly colder serving temperature and versatile fizz add an extra tactile dimension and freshness, while scouring the palate in place of the traditional ginger.

A fun way to serve sushi at parties! Serve with Champagne, or see the wine selection comments on page 105.

BITE-SIZED SUSHI APPETIZERS

SERVES 10 to 15

7 cups sushi rice (see page 113)

12 fresh medium shrimp

1 fresh squid, about 5 ½ ounces (150 g) (see page 116)

5 ½ ounces (150 g) tuna fillet

5 ½ ounces (150 g) salmon fillet

½ avocado

3 crab legs (or imitation crabsticks)

1 cucumber

4 tablespoons ikura salmon roe

6 steamed mussels

3 tablespoons tobikko

2 tablespoons tonburi (or caviar)

Shell and devein the shrimp. Cut the squid, tuna, salmon, and avocado into bite-sized pieces. Pull the crabmeat from the crab legs and roughly chop. Slice the cucumber. Fill small glasses about half full with sushi rice, and top with various combinations of the seafood and other toppings.

SWEET STEAMED EEL ONIGIRI

SERVES 8

½ pack Japanese sweet kabayaki
    eel, about 5 ounces (140 g)

2 cups mochi rice

2 cups water

3 ½ tablespoons soy sauce

2 teaspoons sugar

Cut the eel into ½-inch (1 cm) square pieces. Soak the mochi rice for 30 minutes. Drain and place in a microwave-safe dish with the water, eel, soy sauce, and sugar, and mix well. Cover, and microwave for 13 minutes. Leave to stand, covered, for 5 minutes, and then mix well. Form into egg-sized balls and serve.

For the traditional steaming method, see page 114.

Châteauneuf du Pape
Côtes du Rhône

Typically, grilled eel without any sauce can be matched with a full-bodied Champagne or rosé from Provence. By itself, eel is oily, and when combined with soy sauce and sugar as here, it is best matched with a full-bodied red with softer rounder tannins. While Châteauneuf du Pape is a blend of grapes (up to thirteen varieties are permitted), the predominant variety is Grenache, which gives body, fruitiness, high alcohol, and a glycerine "fatness," and also matures quickly, so it is an ideal match, especially with a little age. A cheaper alternative could be a well-made Côtes du Rhône.

SOBA NOODLES TOPPED WITH VEGETABLES

SERVES 4

2 cucumbers

2 carrots

1 package soba noodles, about
   6 ounces (170 g)

$^1/_2$ tablespoon wasabi

SAUCE

$^1/_4$ cup soy sauce

$^1/_4$ cup mirin

1 cup dashi stock (see page 114)

1 teaspoon sugar

$^1/_4$ cup katsuobushi

To make the sauce, combine the soy sauce, mirin, dashi, and sugar in a saucepan, and bring to a boil. Add the katsuobushi, bring to a boil again, and remove from heat. When the katsuobushi sinks to the bottom of the pot, strain carefully, and discard the katsuobushi. Allow the strained sauce to cool. Thinly slice the cucumbers and carrots using a vegetable peeler. Bring a large pan of water to a boil and add the soba. Use a pair of chopsticks to gently stir the soba and keep it from sticking together. When the pot is about to boil over, add 2 cups water, bring to a boil again, and add 2 more cups water. Take a bite of one strand of soba. It is done when the center is no longer hard. Place the soba in a colander, rinse with cold water, and gently rub with your hands to make it less powdery. Drain well. Arrange the soba on a serving dish and top with the vegetables. Just before eating, pour the sauce over it, and serve with a small amount of wasabi.

Riesling
Grüner Veltliner

As a whole, this dish has very gentle flavors, the only flash-point being the wasabi. Once again, a halbtrocken, or half-dry, Riesling provides a good foil. It has enough weight and character and also, importantly, a fresh acidity inherent in the variety. The acidity helps lift the mild flavors of this dish, and complements it with citrus flavors. If you show restraint with the wasabi, Grüner Veltliner offers an interesting alternative. The carrots, in particular, match up well with this variety.

CHIRIMENJAKO AND PINE NUT ONIGIRI

SERVES 6

6 cups cooked rice (see page 113)

1 teaspoon olive oil

4 ounces (110 g) chirimenjako dried
    fish

1 tablespoon sugar

2 tablespoons mirin

2 tablespoons soy sauce

1 ounce (28 g) pine nuts

Heat the olive oil in a saucepan, add the chirimenjako, and sauté until crispy. Add the sugar, mirin, and soy sauce, and cook until the liquid is absorbed. Add the pine nuts and heat briefly to set the flavor. Remove from heat and allow to cool. Add the rice, and mix through well. Take a handful of mixed rice (about a cup) and press it tightly into a triangular shape.

Lambrusco
Sparkling Wine

My initial instinct was for a Fino sherry to match the pine nuts. On tasting the dish, though, it became obvious that the mirin, soy sauce, and sugar were dominant, therefore needing something slightly sweet to balance it. Here again, a fruity Lambrusco secco filled the slot, with a small amount of residual sugar (10 g/l) to provide the ideal counterbalance. In addition, the bubbles created an extra tactile dimension for the rice ball, which doesn't have a solid, dramatic texture. My second choice was a sparkler from Argentina; dry, but with enough fruity character to balance and match the ingredients of the dish.

HOW TO COOK RICE

Serves 4–6

2 1/2 cups (480 g) rice
3 cups (720 ml) water

First wash the rice. In a large saucepan or bowl, cover the rice with cold water and briefly stir with your hand. Immediately drain off the cloudy water, then add fresh water. Repeat 5 or 6 times or until the water remains clear, then drain well.

To cook the rice, use a saucepan with a tightly fitting lid. Since the rice will expand 2 to 3 times its original volume during cooking, be sure to use a deep enough saucepan. If you like stickier rice, soak the rice ahead of time for up to 30 minutes. Make sure the lid fits securely on the saucepan, then bring the water to a boil and cook on medium heat for 6 to 7 minutes. Reduce the heat to low, and cook for 15 minutes more. Finally, raise the heat to high for about 10 seconds, then remove from heat and let stand for 5 minutes. Use a wooden spatula to stir the rice and allow air into it in order to make it fluffy. If you are not planning to serve the rice immediately, cover it with a dish towel and replace the lid.

If you're lucky enough to have an automatic rice cooker, simply wash and soak the rice as above, then follow the instruction manual.

1 cup (6 3/4 ounces, 190 g) dried rice will produce 3 1/2 cups (15 ounces, 420g) cooked rice.

HOW TO COOK SUSHI RICE

Serves 4–6

2 1/2 cups (480 g) rice
2 1/2 cups (720 ml) water
1 sheet konbu, 4 inches (10 cm) square

4 tablespoons vinegar
3 tablespoons sugar
2 teaspoons salt

Wash and soak the rice, then drain. Make 1/2-inch (1 cm) cuts along each side of the konbu, and soak in the water for about 1 hour. Place the rice in a large saucepan or rice cooker. Remove the konbu pieces from the water and discard, then add the water to the rice and cook according to the instructions for rice, above. Combine the vinegar, sugar, and salt in a small bowl, then add to the cooked rice and mix thoroughly.

3 1/2 cups sushi rice will produce about 12 Nigirizushi (page 102).

TRADITIONAL MOCHI RICE STEAMING METHOD

Use the ingredients for Sweet Steamed Eel Onigiri (page 109). To steam mochi rice only, simply use the rice and water.

Wash the mochi rice and soak overnight. Drain, place in a bowl, and add the water, soy sauce, and sugar. Let stand for 30 minutes, then drain the rice and retain about 2 fluid ounces (50 ml) of the liquid. Cut the eel into ½ inch (1 cm) pieces and mix with the rice. Cover the base of a steaming pan with water, until about ⅔ of the water compartment only (not of the whole pan) is filled. Place the steaming tray on top. Dampen a muslin cloth and wring out well, then use to line the steaming tray. Place the rice and eel onto the cloth. Cover, and fold the edges of the muslin cloth over the top of the steaming pan lid. Steam for 30 to 40 minutes, sprinkling the rice with the retained liquid every 10 minutes.

HOW TO MAKE KONBU DASHI STOCK

The best quality konbu (a type of kelp) is thick and broad (thinner, smaller pieces are generally to be avoided). It should be hard and inflexible, a sign that it has been properly dried. It should have a good fragrance and a dark green color. Avoid yellowish or black konbu as the flavor will be inferior.

Konbu often has white grains on its surface: this is mannitol, an element of its flavor, the so-called umami or "fifth taste." The essential component of this is glutamic acid, which highlights the flavor of the inosinic acid contained in katsuobushi, the other ingredient used to make dashi stock. When using konbu to make dashi stock, dampen a cloth and wring it out tightly, then gently wipe the konbu with it. Do not rinse konbu in water, as this will wash away the mannitol and spoil the flavor.

Konbu should be stored in a cool, dry place in an airtight container. It's handy to cut it into 4 inch (10 cm) square sheets ready for use.

Konbu Dashi Stock   Serves 4

4 inch (10 cm) square sheet konbu
4 cups water

Wipe the konbu, and make ½-inch (1-cm) cuts along each side in order to release the flavor. Put the konbu and water into a saucepan and let stand for about 10 minutes, then heat gently on low. Just before the water boils, remove from heat. Do not allow the water to boil, as this will spoil the flavor. Overcooking the konbu will make the dashi stock slimy.

HOW TO MAKE KATSUOBUSHI DASHI STOCK

Katsuobushi is bonito that has had the skin and entrails removed, and then been dried. Paper-thin flakes of this dried fish are used in many Japanese dishes. The best way to use katsuobushi is to buy the whole fish and shave off the flakes when needed. You can tell the quality of whole katsubushi by striking two pieces together: they should make a clear high-pitched sound. Outside Japan, however, it is probably easiest to buy packets of katsuobushi flakes.

Katsuobushi Dashi Stock   Serves 4

4 cups konbu dashi stock
1 1/4–1 1/2 ounces (35–40 g) katsuobushi flakes

In a medium-sized saucepan, heat the konbu dashi stock. Just before it boils, add the katsuobushi flakes and, without covering, boil for 2 to 3 minutes. Remove from heat. Once the katsuobushi flakes have sunk to the bottom of the pan, strain the liquid through a fine sieve into another container. Do not stir or squeeze the katsuobushi flakes as this will give it a fishy smell!

HOW TO PREPARE FISH

When preparing fish, it is a good idea to cover the chopping board with newspaper in order to avoid the fishy smell from permeating it.

Cleaning
If there is any slime on the fish, this is easily removed by rubbing it with salt and then rinsing it off. To remove the scales, hold the fish down firmly and scrape the blade of a sharp kitchen knife from the tail towards the head, against the grain of the scales.① Turn the fish over and repeat on the other side. Some fish have a line of hard scales extending from the tail: these can be removed with a sharp kitchen knife using a sawing motion.② Insert the tip of the knife into the gill slit and remove the gills.③ Just below the gills, make a 3 to 4-inch (7–10cm) cut with a sharp knife along the belly ④ and remove the entrails.⑤ Rinse well with cold water.

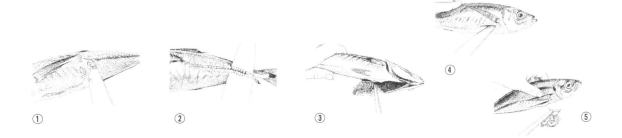

①   ②   ③   ④   ⑤

FILLETING

After following the above steps, place the fish with the head facing to the left. Remove the head,⑥ then insert the knife just above the backbone and run it slowly down to the tail ⑦ to separate the fillet from the bone (ni-mai oroshi). Repeat for the other side (san-mai oroshi).⑧ ⑨

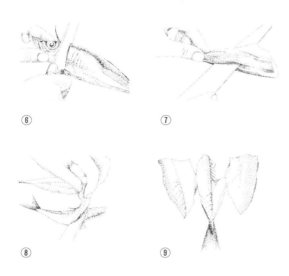

⑥ ⑦

⑧ ⑨

HOW TO PREPARE SQUID

Pull the head portion (which includes the legs) away from the body, and carefully pull out the sac containing the entrails.① Pull out the soft backbone (it looks like a transparent straw).② Grip the triangular mantle and pull it firmly away from the body.③ This leaves the tube-shaped body, open at one end. Remove the skin using a paper towel ④ and rinse the body. If you wish to use the legs, cut them away from the head before discarding the head, entrails, backbone, and mantle.

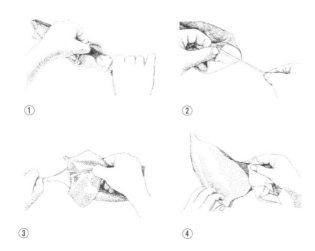

① ②

③ ④

GLOSSARY

Most of these ingredients are generally available in Asian grocery stores and online shopping sites. Substitute ingredients have been indicated where possible.

amaebi
A small sweet shrimp popular for sushi.

chirimenjako
These are small dried fish (anchovies) about ½ inch (1cm) long. They are often available in Asian markets, but may be substituted with the small dried shrimps that are more widely available.

daikon
A giant white radish, generally around 14 inches (35 cm) long and 3 inches (8 cm) thick, with a mildly pungent flavor.

dashi
Stock used in many Japanese recipes (see page 114).

edamame
Fresh soybeans in the pod. They are usually boiled in the pod, but only the bean itself is eaten.

enoki
Clumps of tiny white mushrooms on a long, thin stalk (*Flammulina velutipes*). They are sometimes sold canned or in bottles, or packed fresh in plastic containers.

eringi
A thick stalked cultivated mushroom (*Pleurotus eryngii*) with a flat head, also known as "king oyster mushroom."

hajikami
Pickled ginger shoots, available in bottled form in Asian markets. Other types of pickled ginger may be substituted.

ikura
Salmon eggs, sometimes called salmon caviar.

kabayaki eel
Eel that has been deboned and skewered, then grilled while being basted with a thick, sweet sauce.

kabocha
This Japanese squash resembles a small pumpkin. It may be substituted with pumpkin, although its flesh is slightly darker and denser than an American pumpkin.

katsuobushi
Dried bonito flakes (see page 115).

kinome sprigs
These are the edible young leaves of *sanshō*, or Japanese prickly ash. As a garnish, they may be substituted with mint or basil leaves.

kochijan
Korean soy bean paste made with hot red pepper.

kogomi
A type of edible bracken, also known as "ostrich fern."

konbu
A kelp, or seaweed, that is extensively used in Japanese cooking, particularly for dashi stock (see page 114). Dried konbu is available in Asian supermarkets.

maitake
An autumn mushroom (*Grifola frondosa*), well-known for its health benefits.

mirin
A sweet rice liqueur used exclusively for cooking. It is sometimes referred to as "sweet sake," but this is misleading since, unlike saké, it is made with distilled spirits. It is worth spending a little extra for good-quality mirin ("hon mirin"), which gives a far better flavor than the cheaper varieties.

miso
Soybean paste, used in the preparation of soup and other dishes, and as a condiment.

mizuna
A tender green leaf lettuce, also known as pot herb mustard despite its mild flavor which is similar to ruccola.

mochi rice
Glutinous rice, used for mochi rice cakes and also for some rice dishes.

naganegi
A long green onion resembling a leek. It may be substituted with scallion, green onion, spring onion, or tender leek, depending on the recipe.

rāyu hot pepper oil
Sesame oil spiced with chili peppers.

shichimi seven-spice pepper
Called *shichimi tōgarashi* in Japanese, this is chili pepper with other spices added. It is available at Asian supermarkets, but may be substituted with chili pepper.

shiitake
A large, brown mushroom (*Lentinus edodes*), sometimes known as "golden oak." It is widely available in dried form: simply soak in water before using in cooking.

shimeji
A light, straw-colored mushroom (*Lyophyllum*) with a cap about 1cm in diameter, also known as "oyster mushroom."

shishitō
This is a small, sweet green pepper which looks rather like a green chili, but has a flavor similar to a green bell pepper.

shiso
Perilla. This is a member of the mint family, with a distinctive flavor with overtones of basil as well as mint. The green leaf is most commonly used in cooking, and is often served raw with sashimi or sushi, whereas the red leaf is used to flavor umeboshi pickled plums.

soba
Noodles made from buckwheat.

sudachi
A small citrus fruit with a distinctive flavor, similar to yuzu (see below).

tobikko
Roe of the *tobiuo* Japanese flying fish, this orange caviar is popular with sushi, and is available in jars in delis or Asian food stores.

tonburi
The seed of the broom cypress (*Kochia scoparia*), popular for its tangy taste and crunchy texture, and known in Japan as "land caviar." Its extract is commonly used in Chinese medicine, but the fresh seed is not widely available outside Japan. May best be substituted with caviar.

umeboshi
Dried, salt-pickled Japanese plums (actually a species of apricot) used as a food and condiment. It is also well-known for its health benefits.

wasabi
A pungent, aromatic radish that is grated and used as a condiment mainly for sashimi, sushi, and soba. Tubes of wasabi paste are now widely available in Asian stores.

yamaimo
A type of yam that in Japan is generally served grated, which produces a very slippery texture.

yuzu
A small citrus fruit with a distinctive flavor. Both the rind and the juice are used. It may be substituted with other citrus fruits, such as lime, but the different flavor will significantly affect the flavor of the final dish.

yuzu pepper paste
Called *yuzu koshō* in Japanese, it is sold in small jars in Asian stores.

INDEX

編集協力	ウィラハン・麻未
料理アシスタント	春原幸子
	川田ノリ子
	舛田裕子
AD & DTP	講談社インターナショナル　デザイン室
ワイン提供・協力	ピーロート・ジャパン株式会社

ワインと楽しむ和のレシピ
Japanese Dishes for Wine Lovers

2005年2月25日　第1刷発行

著　者	千葉真知子　　ワイン・コメンテーター　J. K. ウィラハン
撮　影	浜村多恵
訳　者	エリザベス・フロイド
発行者	畑野文夫
発行所	講談社インターナショナル株式会社
	〒112-8652 東京都文京区音羽 1-17-14
	電話　03-3944-6493 （編集部）
	03-3944-6492 （営業部・業務部）
	ホームページ　www.kodansha-intl.com
印刷・製本所	大日本印刷株式会社

落丁本・乱丁本は購入書店名を明記のうえ、講談社インターナショナル業務部宛に
お送りください。送料小社負担にてお取替えいたします。なお、この本についての
お問い合わせは、編集部宛にお願いいたします。本書の無断複写（コピー）は著作権
法の例外を除き、禁じられています。

定価はカバーに表示してあります。